Sawyer Think

Praise for *Sawyer Think*

I have never come across a company more impactful or generous than Sawyer. Kurt Avery is revolutionizing the way that business can change the world. *Sawyer Think* is a blueprint for a better planet.

-Jennifer Pharr Davis,
National Geographic Adventurer and past member of the President's Council for Sports, Fitness, and Nutrition

In the pages of *Sawyer Think*, you will read many terms from the business world and learn recipes for success from someone who has achieved it in abundance. But most importantly you will read about the heart of a man who had dreamed of a business, started a business, suffered through the business, and grew that business to give away 90 percent of the profits—to help others. Most of these people he will never meet on this side of eternity. "For where your treasure is, there your heart will be also" (Matthew 6:21).

-Christopher Beth,
chief storyteller | The Bucket Ministry

I have had the privilege of working with Kurt since 2007. *Sawyer Think* is a close second to learning these valuable principles directly from the source.

-Amy Stead,
key account manager, Sawyer Products

Kurt does an incredible job weaving together the story of Sawyer's growth, the impact that Sawyer has made around the world, and his own unique approach to marketing and decision-making. While some of Kurt's business practices may be considered unorthodox, you will marvel at his unique business framework as you discover true diamonds that you won't be able to find in any other business text.

-Dr. Andrew Babyak,
assistant dean of Business, Messiah University

Kurt is a big thinker who raises the bar on successful business principles that lead to a higher level of Corporate Responsibility that is literally changing the world. This book will not only help your organization grow but will challenge you to maximize your impact in the world through a culture of transformational generosity.

-Darrel Larson,
international director, Humanitarian Programs at Sawyer Products, founder and director at Give Clean Water, and international outreach pastor at Newbreak Church

Kurt Avery has been a living example of the hands and feet of Christ at Hope College. He, along with his wife Barbara, is changing the world one life (or filter) at a time. Hope College and our student-athletes and staff are just one small example of what a life fully surrendered to the Lord can do for the kingdom. As you read *Sawyer Think*, you will see how God has used Kurt to impact lives all over the world and be inspired to use your gifts in similar ways.

-Tim Schoonveld,
director of Athletics, Hope College

Having known Kurt for many years and shared countless hours discussing business, I can confidently say that *Sawyer Think* perfectly encapsulates truly how he thinks and succeeds in business. *Sawyer Think* showcases Kurt's innovative thinking, resilience, and ability to align business goals with a higher mission. Whether you're just starting out or you're a seasoned leader looking to bring more purpose and passion into your business, this book is a must-read. It provides the tools and mindset necessary to drive success and inspire meaningful change in your organization and beyond.

-Don Rice Jr.,
owner of Rice Leadership Group.

Sawyer Think is an engaging volume that tells the story of Kurt Avery's distinctive approach to utilizing business principles not solely for the purpose of making a profit but to do good—using profits to make a difference in the lives of the underserved. The rich discussion of decision-making and marketing principles is interwoven with compelling real-world anecdotes that demonstrate the truly global impact of *Sawyer Think*. Leaders in every sector—from business and nonprofits to higher education—will benefit greatly from reading Avery's book.

-Kim S. Phipps, Ph.D.,
president of Messiah University in Mechanicsburg, PA

Sawyer Think is a challenging, inspiring, world-changing story! A powerful example of how we can't out-give God, Sawyer has generously re-invested their resources. We can only hope it inspires others to follow their lead!

-Aaron Faro,
sports ministry director &
associate head men's soccer coach, Messiah University

Sawyer® THINK

How a Small Company Disrupts Markets and Changes the World

KURT AVERY

NEW YORK
LONDON • NASHVILLE • MELBOURNE • VANCOUVER

Sawyer Think

How a Small Company Disrupts Markets and Changes the World

© 2025 Kurt Avery & A.L. Rogers

All rights reserved. No portion of this book may be reproduced, stored in a retrieval system, or transmitted in any form or by any means—electronic, mechanical, photocopy, recording, scanning, or other—except for brief quotations in critical reviews or articles, without the prior written permission of the publisher.

Published in New York, New York, by Morgan James Publishing. Morgan James is a trademark of Morgan James, LLC. www.MorganJamesPublishing.com

Proudly distributed by Publishers Group West®

Scriptures taken from the Holy Bible, New International Version®, NIV®. Copyright © 1973, 1978, 1984, 2011 by Biblica, Inc.™ Used by permission of Zondervan. All rights reserved worldwide. www.zondervan.com. The "NIV" and "New International Version" are trademarks registered in the United States Patent and Trademark Office by Biblica, Inc.™

Morgan James BOGO™

A **FREE** ebook edition is available for you or a friend with the purchase of this print book.

CLEARLY SIGN YOUR NAME ABOVE

Instructions to claim your free ebook edition:
1. Visit MorganJamesBOGO.com
2. Sign your name CLEARLY in the space above
3. Complete the form and submit a photo of this entire page
4. You or your friend can download the ebook to your preferred device

ISBN 9781636985473 paperback
ISBN 9781636985480 ebook
Library of Congress Control Number: 2024942584

Cover & Interior Design by:
Christopher Kirk
www.GFSstudio.com

Morgan James is a proud partner of Habitat for Humanity Peninsula and Greater Williamsburg. Partners in building since 2006.

Get involved today! Visit: www.morgan-james-publishing.com/giving-back

Contents

Introduction 1

Chapter One | What You Must Know to Even Start
   a Business 7
Chapter Two | Creative Destruction. 29
Chapter Three | Financing the Business 45
Chapter Four | Managing the Business 63
Chapter Five | Making Decisions 81
Chapter Six | The Decision Matrix 91
Chapter Seven | The Circle of Customers 109
Chapter Eight | Turning Your Customers into Partners . . 127
Chapter Nine | Protecting Your Business for
   Future Growth 149
Chapter Ten | Packaging and More 171
Chapter Eleven | Incremental Variable Cost 185
Chapter Twelve | Think Big. 205

Acknowledgments 223

About the Author 225
Glossary 227
Appendices 231

Introduction

On January 12, 2010, a 7.0-magnitude earthquake struck Haiti. An estimated 220,000 people were killed and 1,500,000 people became homeless. The capital city, Port-au-Prince, was left in rubble. It all happened in a matter of minutes.

At the time, Haiti was one of the poorest countries in the world. Bodies were left in the street or under piles of debris. Injuries went untreated and became worse. Cholera and typhoid soon followed. People sat in the ruin with nowhere to go and no resources to meet their needs. There was also no safe, clean water available for drinking or medical use. Sawyer Products was able to supply more than one hundred thousand water filters without missing a beat in our manufacturing. We estimate that these filters could have impacted up to two million lives. It was the first major event to establish what our filter could really do.

On September 7, 2017, Puerto Rico was hit by Hurricane Irma, a Category 5 storm. Less than two weeks later, on September 20, Puerto Rico was hit *again* by Hurricane Maria, a Category 4 storm. This deadly combination cost thousands of lives and devasted Puerto Rico's fragile infrastructure, leaving survivors without power or clean water. Due to landslides, rainfall saturation, and inoperable waste treatment plants, experts estimated that 95 percent of people in Puerto Rico lacked drinking water in the immediate aftermath of the storm.[1] Now in much better financial shape, Sawyer Products donated, or sold at a deep discount, more than one hundred thousand additional water filters. Again, enough to meet the needs of another two million people.

We learned through this experience that, while both earthquakes and hurricanes are devastating, hurricanes provide advance warning of their arrival. Many non-governmental organizations (NGOs) took suitcases full of Sawyer water filters to Puerto Rico ahead of the storms because they knew clean water would be needed as soon as the storms moved on.

Since 2008, when Sawyer first began participating with other organizations in relief efforts, we estimate that we've been able to impact *twenty-eight million people* (and counting) by providing access to clean drinking water. We have 140 charitable partners, and we participate in relief efforts for nearly every major natural disaster, as well as relief efforts in numerous war zones and military conflicts. Plus, we have transformational distribution to families, schools, and orphanages in more than eighty countries. In recent years, we have been able to give away 90 percent of our profits through Sawyer, the Sawyer Foundation, and other charitable efforts.

---

1   "Hurricanes Irma and Maria: Impact and Aftermath," RAND, accessed October 13, 2023, https://www.rand.org/hsrd/hsoac/projects/puerto-rico-recovery/hurricanes-irma-and-maria.html.

These numbers are *staggering*. I am not opening the book with them to brag or take credit. I marvel at them too. When I started the company in the 1980s, I could never have imagined the impact that Sawyer products would someday have on real lives—twenty-eight million of them—around the world. Never in my wildest dreams would I have guessed that our little company, which began with a niche product that removed bug and snake venom, would become such a global force in the quest for clean water. Nor would I have envisioned a day when we would give away such a high percentage of our profit.

So how did we get here? How did a relatively small company in Florida become a world leader in water filtration? How did we become "more than an outdoor company" and get to the point where we can donate tens of thousands of water filters every year, anywhere around the world, without feeling any pressure on our viability? What are the business practices that enable us to be so generous? And why do we give so much away in the first place?

I am asked these questions a lot. I'm going to attempt to answer them in this book with the hopes that you will take my answers back into your organization and begin to change the world too.

In addition to stories about Sawyer's role in relief efforts around the world (and boy, do we have some incredible stories to share!) I'm also going to be talking about marketing, economics, and leadership. I'm going to show you how we became successful in our market and able to make the money we now give away.

Why? Because I'm a marketer. When I introduce myself to people, I like to keep it simple. I don't want fanfare or hoopla.

I don't introduce myself as the president of this or that or the founder of yadda yadda. I say, "I'm a marketer," "Call me Kurt," and "I serve a big God." (If you're not a person of faith, don't worry. This book is not a sermon. However, my Christian faith is an integral part of my "why" and also part of Sawyer's success, so it's going to come up from time to time.)

Before I started Sawyer, I was a country boy, a Little League slugger, a baseball card-collecting math nut, and eventually a marketing guy for some globally known brands you'll probably recognize. We're going to talk about all of those things too. I'll try not to bore you with these stories. (The things Sawyer is doing around the world are more interesting anyway.)

In this book, we're going to focus on two big ideas: *maximizing your business potential* and *changing the world*. By walking through what some have called "Sawyer Think" (not my term, but I like it!), I hope to pass on the marketing and economic principles that disrupted the markets of insect repellents and water filters and ultimately built Sawyer Products into the company it is today. By sharing stories from our relief work around the world—many of which come from the excellent team of on-the-ground people we have at Sawyer—I hope to inspire you to take a radically different approach to profits and change the world with your organization.

As you read this book, you will see that I am not a detail person. I am a macro thinker, the big picture, the thirty-thousand-foot-view person. Most important and pivotal decisions do not require great detail. So, if you are a detail person, this book will be good for you because it will help you think differently than you often do. If you're like me and you're not a detail person, this book will be comfortable for you. But I warn you that if you are not a detail person, make sure you have detail people on your staff. Your production line will be shut down if you forget to order all the parts needed. You won't be able to make all the items on your menu if you don't buy all the ingredients. You could also have IRS or bank problems if you don't have accountants minding the details.

Businesses flourish best when they have both detail and non-detail people working together. However, it is probably best to have the non-detail people make the strategic decisions while being fact-checked by the detail people.

Sawyer Think is a mix of core marketing principles, some lesser-known techniques that we rely on heavily at Sawyer, and radical decisions about how to use the profit. I'm going to challenge you to think *big*. I'm going to ask you to think about how you and your company can solve *big* problems. As I said, I never could've dreamed that Sawyer Products would become what it is today. But I serve a *big* God and I'm surrounded by incredible people. Let me tell you some of their stories.

Chapter One

What You Must Know to Even Start a Business

What are you good at? I'm serious. What are you *really good* at? You probably feel passionate about something. You probably have a big idea that you want to share with the world. These are good things, but before you start your business, you need to do a heart-to-heart inventory of your skill set. You must understand what you're good at.

When I started Sawyer, I knew I was good at marketing. I always have been. I have an underlying belief that marketing is really just the study of human behavior. We use marketing tools to understand people and find our sweet spots in whatever sphere we operate within. I learned this lesson early and it has never left me.

What are you *not* good at? Sometimes you need other people to help you answer this question, others who will be honest with you. Whatever it is that you can't do, it is not the limiting factor you might think it is. But when you start a business, you build on what you *can* do. Then you fill in what you can't do with other talented people.

Since Sawyer began, I have hired people to do many things because there are many things I can't do. But I know what I can do, marketing being one of them. Now here is the fun part: *marketers make all the money*. It's true! This is not simply marketing bias from a marketing guy. Marketers bring it all in.

Engineers design all the products. (Sawyer has some incredible engineers on staff. I will introduce you to the engineer who designed the first Sawyer water filters later.) But in my experience, engineers don't know how to stop engineering. They are always dabbling and trying to improve things.

Accountants are too rigid. They're counting the beans but they don't know how to think of opportunities unless it's within accounting. They might start a new accounting firm or come up with the next QuickBooks, but generally, they don't think of ideas outside the box.

This brings us back to marketing. Why do marketers make all the money? Because marketing is the bridge between your big idea—whatever that thing is that you're passionate about—and the purchase.

Sawyer is a marketing machine. We are constantly building bridges to our customers and the bridges work both ways. Marketing isn't about just blasting *out* messages, it's about taking them in too. We listen to what consumers want and then we go find a solution.

In this chapter, I will describe what I see as a baseline understanding that everyone must have before starting a business. These baseline principles are just as much a part of "Sawyer Think" as any of the truly unique ideas we'll get into later. Many of them have to do with marketing.

For some of you, the following information will be old. You learned it while studying for your undergraduate degree in business or during your MBA program. If that's you, feel free to skip to the next chapter or enjoy this brief review. But there are a lot of people in business who aren't aware of these fundamental concepts. I've met countless entrepreneurs who are driven by a passion for their product or service, yet they are clueless about the fundamentals of running a good business. If that's you, there's nothing to be embarrassed about. Everyone needs to learn the core principles at some point. This is your time.

The Four Ps of Marketing

The Four Ps of Marketing are product, presence, promotion, and pricing. We will discuss each of them briefly. Specifically, we are going to focus on the information you must have if you want to get your business off the ground.

Product

Having a product that people actually want and need is key to success. Before you build your business around a new widget, ask yourself these fundamental questions: Does it solve a market problem? Does it address an opportunity?

> Having a product that people actually want and need is key to success.

When Sawyer released its first consumer-grade permethrin insect repellent in 1991, we were able to say yes in response to both of these questions. The market problem was that topical repellents are designed for use on the skin and only last for one day or less. What if we could treat fabric (clothes, tents, backpacks, etc.) and have that one treatment last for weeks? Permethrin does that, so there is a market for it. The opportunity was not only to meet a need but also to provide a whole new option (permethrin) for the early educator and early innovator consumers we targeted. Permethrin is a staple for US military uniforms. We asked ourselves, how might civilians benefit from it as well?

Presence

Presence is about your channels of distribution and any coming changes. Identifying your channels of distribution is the first step. Everyone will tell you that these have changed drastically over the last thirty or more years. Amazon and other online retailers have changed everything.

But identifying your current channels of distribution is the easy part. The more challenging aspect of *presence* is to *avoid looking at today and instead focus on tomorrow.* Here's what I mean: Imagine that you want to open a new restaurant. You spend a great deal of time focusing on a unique concept and a great location. You open and you begin serving Baby Boomers, Gen X, and millennials. Then Gen Z shows up and likes your food but prefers to order via Uber Eats, DoorDash, or some other delivery service. Your concept is not quite built for that. What do you do?

In this book, we're going to talk a lot about the importance of future thinking. In the context of this chapter, as we discuss the process of launching a new business, the big idea about presence is simply *don't look at today.* Think about what channels of distribution—your presence—will be needed tomorrow.

Promotion

Advertising, public relations, email campaigns, social media, your sales force—all fall under the category of promotion. Identifying the optimum promotional vehicles for your target market is your primary task.

A great place to start is to identify where you are on the bell curve. Sawyer aims for the early educators and early innovators (sometimes called early adopters). This means that if you look at a bell curve based on the psychological or social segmentation of consumers, our target market is on the right side of the curve, i.e., people who want more features and innovations.

Consumer Bell Curve

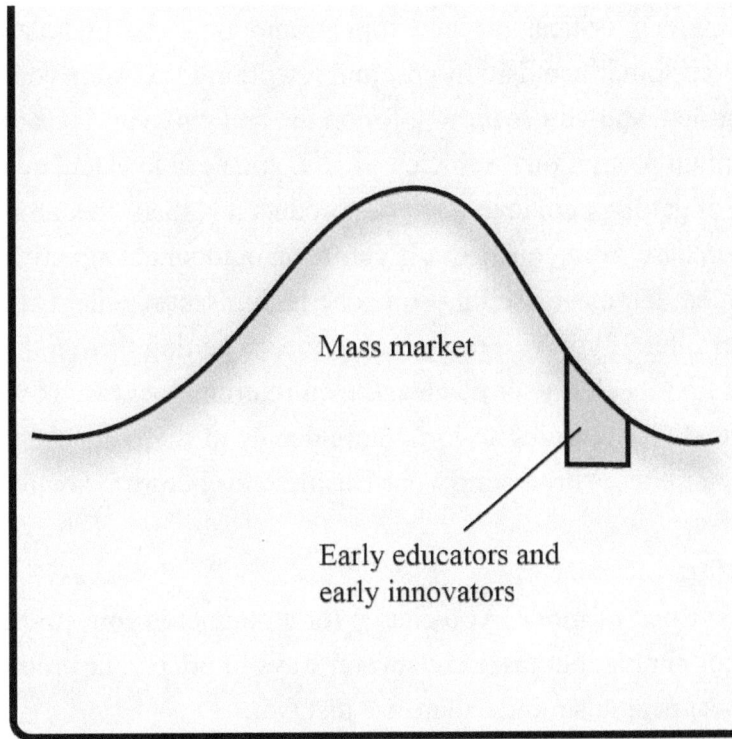

For Sawyer, these optimum promotional opportunities change over time. Social media has become the optimum vehicle for our products. Why? Because the early educators and early innovators we're aiming for are frequently watching video reviews from notable influencers in the hiking and camping world. If we want to launch a new insect repellent, we'll focus our efforts on getting those critical reviews on the right social media channels. It would do us no good whatsoever to run something like a Super Bowl ad. The big brand, DEET-based insect repellents might run an ad there, but they're aiming for a different consumer. They're trying to get the average person walking through a drugstore to pick up a can of spray on the way to a day at the park. We're aiming for the hiker or camper who is going to spend all day or week deep in the woods.

Another critical piece within promotion is to understand your customer acquisition cost and retention rate. After you've identified who you're aiming for on the bell curve and what the optimum promotional vehicles will be, you need to calculate the cost of getting people to buy your product and then stick around to purchase from you again. If you're an outdoors company like Sawyer, that means selling someone both insect repellent and a water filter. If you're a restaurant, it means getting them to have their first meal at your place and then returning next week with a friend. We're going to look more deeply at these concepts in Chapter Nine, "Protecting Your Business for Future Growth."

Pricing

The amount of money you charge for a product is your price. It sounds simple, but there are several ways to price your product. In most people's minds, there are just two.

First, people will think, I've made the widget for ten dollars and I want a 50 percent margin, so I'm going to sell it for twenty dollars. That's fine. This is a profit-based pricing model. But what if the people will pay thirty dollars? This is about understanding the value of a product, not just pricing according to your profit goal.

For instance, a two-liter bottle of soda probably costs about ten to twelve cents to make. Then it might cost another dime per bottle to ship it to the store. Yet, most people are willing to pay $1.69 or more for a two-liter bottle of soda. Why? Because *you're willing* to pay $1.69, and because the soda company uses that extra money for Super Bowl ads and other campaigns.

Conversely, you might work with an engineer who designs a great new widget. She may believe it's worth fifty dollars, but then after running focus groups and consumer studies, you discover that most people won't give you more than twenty dollars for it. No matter how great the new widget is, sometimes consumers may not be willing to pay what you think is a great deal.

So, you should always ask yourself, what is this worth to the customer? Is it worth more than I need to charge (like the soda)? Or is it worth less to them than you realize (like the engineer's widget)? Your choices are to either better explain the features and their benefits (you sell features, people buy benefits) and thus increase their value perception, lower your cost to meet their perceptions, or abandon the product.

Another pricing model to think about early on is short-term/long-term pricing. This pricing model is about forcing greater volume by making your product inexpensive.

In 2005, we released an amazing new water filter, the Sawyer Squeeze Water Filtration System. The filters we were replacing sold for seventy to eighty dollars. We could've charged seventy or eighty dollars and people probably would've switched because our filter was lighter, faster, and better. But at that price, we were likely to sell the same number of water filters as our competition. So instead, we priced our new filter at $29.95 in order to get a whole new set of consumers.

At first, retailers were upset. I remember one person saying, "I make forty dollars when I sell one of their filters. I'm only going to make ten bucks when I sell one of yours."

"I understand," I responded, "but wait till you see how many you're going to sell." The market had been about seventy thousand units a year at eighty dollars. After our filter was released, it shifted. We were a major disruption in the market. Now the market is more than a million units a year at around twenty to thirty dollars.

What would you rather have for your company? The higher price or the higher volume? The volume! Had we priced our filter at seventy or eighty dollars, we would have never sold it to new customers like the Boy Scouts. A few may have purchased some, but not nearly at the volume we sold. In the end, you spend dollars, not percentages. It is better to make 30 percent on one hundred thousand dollars than 50 percent on ten thousand dollars.

You won't always have opportunities to disrupt the market like this, but as we'll discuss in different ways throughout each chapter, things are always changing. Sometimes these changes will allow you to expand your market by magnitudes. That's short-term/long-term pricing.

Each of the Four P principles has options. You need to figure out which of the options within each principle will combine to work best for you. At Sawyer, we never make any marketing decision without analyzing the Four Ps.

The Five Cs of Marketing

The Five Cs of Marketing are sometimes called the Five Cs Analysis. The purpose of the Five Cs Analysis is to create a distinction, or Point of Difference (POD), between you and your competition. They are a helpful framework for analyzing your operating environment.[2] The Five Cs are:

Company

At the start of any new business, or even at the launch of a new product, you should ask yourself, what gives us an advantage over our competitors? This advantage could come in different forms. It could be in superior technology, lower cost, brand equity (which we'll discuss in depth in Chapter Nine), or any other number of factors. For Sawyer, our advantage begins with higher standards for research, testing, and development than any of our competitors.

Collaborators

Your collaborators are those who help you deliver your good or service. These are your vendors, shipping services, and others in your supply chain. We'll talk more about creating strong relationships with collaborators throughout the book.

---

2 "5C Analysis," Corporate Finance Institute, accessed January 16, 2024, https://corporatefinanceinstitute.com/resources/management/5c-analysis-marketing/.

Customers

Your customers are, of course, those to whom you're selling your goods or services. In this book, we're going to refer to two groups of customers. Group one includes trade partners who are sometimes referred to as retailers or retail partners. Group two includes the end consumers. At Sawyer, we've taken great care to cultivate strong relationships with both trade partners and consumers. We've dedicated full chapters in this book to discussing how to understand your customers (Chapter Seven, "The Circle of Customers") and how to build those important relationships (Chapter Nine, "Turning Your Customers into Partners").

Competitors

Your competitors include anyone operating in the same market with a similar good or service. Understanding your competitors can be as simple or as complex as understanding your customers. We will discuss numerous ways to maintain your competitive edge throughout this book.

Context

Context refers to the political, economic, social, technical, environmental, and legal factors your business operates within. Context is sometimes called "climate" because context is experienced like a natural environment you live in but cannot control. Contextual factors affect your business. We'll take a look at some examples of contextual factors in Chapter Two, "Creative Destruction."

The purpose of the Five C Analysis is to figure out how to separate your product or service from your competitors. If the consumer can't tell the difference, then you become a commodity (gas, sugar, etc.) and you have a race to the lowest price. If you can separate your product or service from the competition due to PODs (points of differences), distinctives, or brand equity, then you can charge a higher price or increase your market share, which means higher profits.

Life Cycle Curves

Knowing where you are at all times on the product life cycle curve is critical for success. There are generally five accepted phases of life cycle curves: introduction, growth, maturity, decline, and long-term stability.

Life Cycle Curves

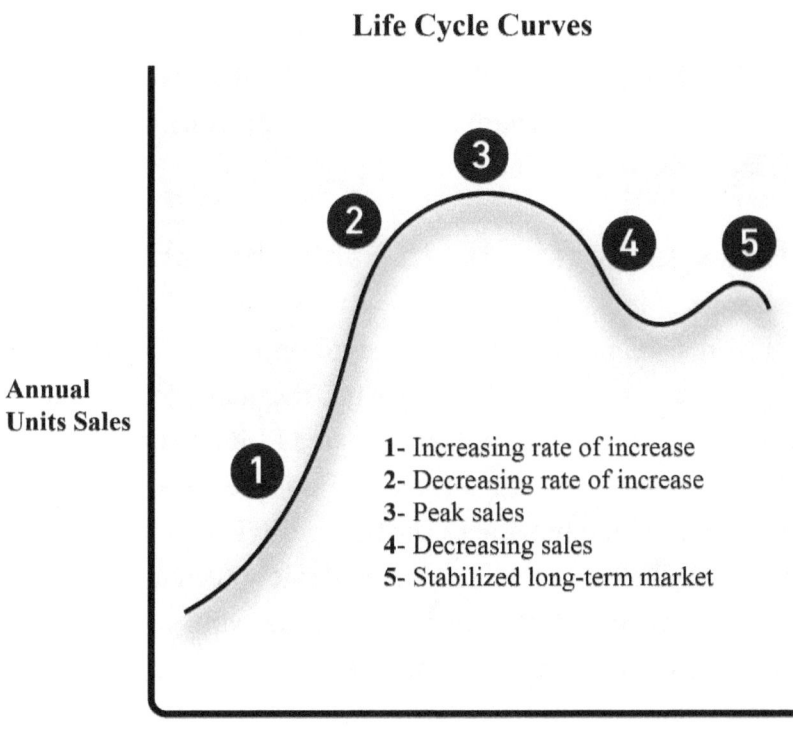

1- Increasing rate of increase
2- Decreasing rate of increase
3- Peak sales
4- Decreasing sales
5- Stabilized long-term market

Each stage influences your strategy—how much you should pay for advertising, how much effort you should put into marketing, when you should consider repackaging, when you should consider increasing production or decreasing production, and selling something new to those customers. We'll discuss the key points listed on this diagram: the increasing rate of increase, the decreasing rate of increase, the peak, decreasing sales, and a stabilized long-term market.

All products will ride this curve. Some will have long periods of maturity (like Cheerios or Coca-Cola), but others will not (like Blu-ray discs). Eventually, all products will phase out and be removed from the market by the manufacturer. Products get phased out because of market saturation, decreased demand, strong competition, and always decreasing sales.

I'll refer to the life cycle curve throughout the book and how understanding where your product is can help you make the best decisions for your business.

PERT Charts: (similar to Gantt Charts)

There are a lot of great online resources about PERT charts, so I'm not going to spend much time on them here. But as a reminder, and to give us a baseline understanding for the rest of the chapter, here's a quick definition of a PERT chart: "A PERT chart is a visual project management tool used to map out and track the tasks and timelines. The name PERT is an acronym for Project (or Program) Evaluation and Review Technique."[3]

When using a PERT chart, you start at your end goal and work backward, planning all the tasks that will need to be com-

---

3 "PERT Chart," ProductPlan, accessed December 19, 2023, https://www.productplan.com/glossary/pert-chart/.

pleted in order to arrive at your goal.[4] This process will reveal the total length of time it's going to take you to get there as well as all of the necessary tasks that need to be completed and in which order they need to be completed. When should you begin marketing? When does your shelving need to arrive? When do you need to have the internet and computers up and running? Should you start advertising this month or next? These are the types of questions that a PERT chart can help you answer.

The PERT chart is a classic business management tool that you need to use in order to make informed decisions. It's also a visual tool, which can be helpful for different learning styles on your team. If you're making a product, start with your launch date and work backward. If you're in retail, food service, or a service industry—opening a coffee house, opening up your repair shop, whatever—start with your grand opening day and work backward. An alternative use would be to ask, "If I started now, when could I be finished?"

Also, when going in either direction, you can identify actions that can be accomplished simultaneously instead of sequentially and thereby shorten the whole timeline. Those in the construction industry are masters at this.

What's in a Name?

Naming a new business can be difficult. So much seems to ride on that one decision. How can you be sure you're picking the right name?

People have asked me over the years where the name *Sawyer* comes from. Most people assume it's one of my names or a

---

[4] PERT charts are similar to one of Stephen Covey's seven habits of highly-effective people, "Begin with the end in mind."

family name. It's not! I'd never name a company after myself. I know it's common to do so, but I wouldn't want to do that to my poor kids. Whether we're successful or a failure, I would not want to force the kids to deal with that.

Our first product was a bee sting and snake bite kit, which we eventually called the Sawyer Extractor™ Pump Kit. I wasn't going to name the company after that one product. Instead, I wanted to go to the market with a biblical name to represent this product. I looked in the Bible but couldn't find something that I really wanted or that would jump out on the shelves. But one particular story about the apostle Paul on the island of Malta caught my attention. In Acts 28, Paul lands safely on the island on a cold and rainy day. While gathering wood for a fire, he is bit by a viper. The local islanders see the snake hanging from his hand and their superstitions are aroused. They assume he must be a murderer to suffer such a dire consequence from one of their local gods. However, Paul simply shakes the snake from his hand and suffers no ill effects. The story ends with God curing the islanders of disease through Paul's prayers.

I liked this story and it was about a snake bite, which seemed like a nice connection to our first product. I felt that Acts 28:4, 5, and 6 were the heart of the story. I took the first letters in the words *Acts twenty-eight four, five, and six* and reversed them to create the name *Saffeta*. That's how the company got its first name. It was a hidden allusion to Scripture and I just liked it.

When I went to my first trade show in 1984, all the messaging was: "Buy American! Buy American! Buy American!" Saffeta didn't sound like a very American name to me. So, I went back to one of my early vendor partners, an artist, and asked, "What's the most American name you can come up with?" Together we landed on Sawyer, like Tom Sawyer, the hero of Mark Twain's great American novel. The artist even designed a logo of Tom Sawyer running.

We immediately shifted to "Saffeta, doing business as Sawyer" on all of the necessary paperwork, and by 1985 we had changed all of our packaging to Sawyer. We used the DBA until 1991, mostly because I liked the old name. Eventually, it made sense to officially change the name of the company. In May of 1988, during the DBA years, we moved the company to Florida. When we first started Saffeta, we were based out of Illinois. Some of our messaging said, "Saffeta, an Illinois Company." That wouldn't be true anymore after the move, so we eventually shifted to "Sawyer, a Florida Company." It was just a natural changeover.

So how do you come up with a name for a new company?

My first piece of advice is to stay away from family names unless the name is part of a celebrity package. As we've discussed, Sawyer is not Avery Inc.

My second piece of advice is to avoid names that will limit your ability to expand laterally. Later in the book, I'm going to share a few lessons I learned while working for Weed Eater. The first lesson we can take from my time there has to do with its name. Weed Eater was named after its first product, which limited their ability to add related products.

For instance, imagine that you open a restaurant and call it Joe's Pizza. Later you add subs, so it becomes Joe's Pizza and Subs. Then it becomes Joe's Pizza, Subs and Salads, etc. If you just start with Joe's or Joe's Italian Restaurant, lateral expansion is much easier. You always have the opportunity to add a subtitle to the name such as Pizza, Subs, Salads, and more.

Bottom line: Think about where you may want to go with your product line and leave room for lateral additions. But be careful that you don't get so abstract that you lose the advantage of a category descriptive name. For instance, the name Dunkin' Donuts was very helpful in getting them started. After billions in sales and thousands of locations, they could with relative ease transition into Dunkin' since they expanded their line and hours.[5]

Putting It All Together

You need to know the Four Ps. You need to know the Five Cs. You need to understand consumer bell curves and product life cycle curves. And working with PERT charts can be incredibly useful for shortening timelines and getting work done. You will find these in every marketing textbook and they are all over the

---

5 "Welcome to Dunkin': Dunkin' Donuts Reveals New Brand Identity," Dunkin' Newsroom, September 25, 2018, https://news.dunkindonuts.com/news/releases-20180925.

internet. I've covered them here just briefly because you must know them for all that will follow in this book. (If you want to dig more deeply into them, you can find them discussed at length in marketing textbooks.) They are the core concepts for the new things we are going to talk about, which you won't find in those other books.

But this book is about more than just business growth. At the end of every chapter, we're going to pause the discussion on business and economics to consider a story of real-world impact. I'm going to relay stories that come from various Sawyer team members and some of our charity partners. Most of the content in this book is about how to grow your business. If you apply the principles of *Sawyer Think*, then I believe you'll see greater profits in your business. But what do you do with all that money? That's what the stories of real-world impact are all about.

The Global Water Crisis

Most people don't realize how bad the global water crisis is. In the "UN World Water Development Report 2023," an annual report on global water and sanitation issues, the following dire facts were reported[6]:

- Twenty-six percent of the world's population, approximately two billion people, do not have access to safe drinking water.
- 3.6 billion people lack access to safe sanitation services.

---

6   "UN World Water Development Report," United Nations, accessed January 12, 2024, https://unesdoc.unesco.org/ark:/48223/pf0000384655.

- "Water scarcity in urban areas is expected to worsen as projections show that projected doubling from 930 million in 2016 to between 1.7 and 2.4 billion people, in 2050."[7]
- Water scarcity has the greatest impact on poorer people and children. (For example, an estimated 70 percent of sub-Saharan Africa lacks safe water.)[8]

The list of data around the global water crisis could go on and on, but to put it simply, those of us in developed countries take clean water for granted. We water our lawns, wash our cars, and flush our toilets with water that others would die for—literally. They would die to have access to the water you use to hose down your automobile. Does that seem extreme? If you consider the water they have available, it is not. We have seen countless locations around the world where people's water sources are contaminated by animal waste, garbage, sediment, debris, runoff, and even human waste.

I did not have the global water crisis in mind when we started Sawyer. But as Sawyer grew over the years, and as we started to carve a name for the company in the water filter market, we could not ignore the global water crisis, nor could we ignore the immediate needs people have for clean water in the aftermath of natural disasters or war. We'll discuss what makes our high-performance water filters the best products in the industry

---

7 "Summary report, 22-24 March 2023," International Institute for Sustainable Development, accessed January 12, 2024, https://enb.iisd.org/un-2023-water-conference-summary.

8 "Global water crisis looming, UN says - BBC News," BBC News, March 22, 2023, https://www.youtube.com/watch?v=hfTB5TgJq5w.

and how we have grown that business in later chapters. But at this point, we need to take a step back and think about water from a global perspective.

What Happens When You Give Someone Clean Water?

At the beginning of this chapter, I asked you to consider the question, "Does your product solve a market problem?" I can say with confidence that Sawyer water filters solve not only a market problem but also health problems associated with the global water crisis. By partnering with various universities, we have been able to research and field test Sawyer water filters in a number of situations. Here are some of the definitive results of giving someone clean water from our published research:

- Calvin University (Grand Rapids, Michigan) studied over 105,000 homes in rural Liberia that received a Sawyer International Bucket Filter system. In a peer-reviewed journal, they published that diarrhea rates dropped from 36 percent to 1.5 percent in these homes.
- In the same study, we learned that children from zero to five years old were nineteen times less likely to get diarrhea, youth from five to seventeen years old were twenty-nine times less likely to get diarrhea, and adults were forty-four times less likely to get diarrhea.
- In another study, Hope College (Holland, Michigan) examined ten thousand homes in the Kibera slum in Nairobi, Kenya. Diarrhea rates in the homes with Sawyer water filters dropped from 54 percent to 2.2 percent.

- Then in 2022, Hope College demonstrated that Sawyer water filters increase worker productivity in a corporate setting. They distributed Sawyer water filters in a Cambodian factory. In addition to diarrhea rates dropping, they learned that each factory worker using a filter saved 2.03 workdays per employee per month. That totals more than two thousand workdays recaptured by the factory each month.[9]

There's more to clean water than diarrhea reduction and worker productivity. Consider that every day people all over the world boil water in order to drink it, cook with it, and clean with it. That's a lot of fossil fuel—and a lot of money—being used for a basic human necessity. So, giving someone access to clean water will affect not only their health but their wallet too. It keeps money in their pocket that they can use for other necessities, often within their local economies. A study by Hope College demonstrated that families in Fiji saved $635 per year after receiving a Sawyer water filter. We call this purchased water savings.

There are anecdotal benefits to giving someone clean water that we're still working to quantify accurately. One example is the overall effect of dehydration. When you have to work so hard for water, you're constantly dehydrated. You see this in the reality show *Survivor* and similar shows all the time. When the contestants are dehydrated, they don't think straight. This is true, of course, for the people who spend their entire lives

---

9 Published Sawyer research can be found at www.sawyer.com/certification. A summary video is also available: "Sawyer Research & Certification," Sawyer Products, October 17, 2023, https://www.youtube.com/watch?v=2asRkP92vqo.

drinking filthy water or working hard to get clean water. The flip side to this reality is that when you give someone access to abundant clean water, they suddenly start to do things they couldn't do otherwise because now they're thinking straight. They become more energetic and entrepreneurial. They start to affect their local communities in positive ways, like starting a new business. While we can't yet quantify these positive effects, they are an undeniable reality. When people are no longer living in a dehydrated state, they are able to thrive in ways they never could have before.

One more anecdotal story: One of the stats above is about the Kibera slum in Nairobi. In another chapter, you're going to learn that, in Kibera, the global water crisis can be seen easily everywhere you look. Kibera is made up of thirteen villages, two estates, and multiple ethnic groups. There have always been tensions between the groups. As clean water efforts have increased the amount of clean water available in Kibera, there has been less friction between the groups. There is still tension, but the violence has gone way down. This is another benefit of clean water that we are still trying to quantify, but the results are again undeniable.

Whether it's a lifelong battle with dehydration, a disease, or tribal unrest, access to clean water removes a huge stressor from someone's life, which has a ripple effect on everything else they do. We have a *big* vision to fight this *big* problem. We didn't know it would be our problem to solve when Sawyer began, but the impact we can make is indisputable. Is there a *big* problem your business can tackle?

Chapter Two
Creative Destruction

The world was at war in 1942 and the war created major changes. Axis powers advanced across Europe and the South Pacific, where they met the Allied forces who fought hard to drive them back. Even for those not on the front lines, everything was touched by war. Consumers spent more on medical bills and food and less on entertainment and housing. Automobile production stopped in favor of manufacturing supplies for the military. Congress signed the Emergency Price Control Act in January of that year, and ration stamps were distributed in an attempt to stabilize the economy.

During that same year, an Austrian economist named Joseph Schumpeter published a book called *Capitalism, Socialism and Democracy* that forever altered how global economics is approached and perceived. Schumpeter argued that industries destroy and create themselves from *within* through innovative developments, often achieved by entrepreneurs who introduce something revolutionary. He said this was an essential fact of capitalism and that it was necessary for economic growth.[10] Through this book, Schumpeter popularized a concept called Creative Destruction.

Now remember, my underlying belief is that marketing is really just the study of human behavior. We use marketing tools to understand our consumers and find the sweet spot for our products. Well, Creative Destruction essentially says *things are going to change*. That means if we want to be marketers, entrepreneurs, and leaders who disrupt their markets and change the world, then we need to *study human behavior and predict how things are going to change*.

Creative Destruction is easy to see in three different spheres—government law, technology, and cultural norms. What happens when any one of these spheres experience Creative Destruction? *Life* changes. Things are destroyed and things are created. Let's take a look at a few examples.

Creative Destruction in Government Law: The Americans with Disabilities Act

The Americans with Disabilities Act of 1990 (ADA) is a civil rights law that prohibits discrimination based on disability.[11] This law required employers to provide reasonable accommodations to employees and customers with disabilities.

At the time, most workplaces were not equipped with ramps, elevators, or other amenities necessary for everyone to

---

10 Joseph A. Schumpeter, *Capitalism, Socialism and Democracy* (London: Routledge,1942). This book is essential reading for anyone who seeks to understand where the world economy is headed.
11 It is similar to the Civil Rights Act of 1964 which prohibited discrimination based on race, religion, gender, ethnicity, and other characteristics.

work, regardless of their ability. The ADA would change that by requiring businesses to increase accessibility for disabled people by building ramps, installing elevators, and providing specialized work equipment. Lawmakers hoped that these changes would increase the number of disabled Americans who were employed.

Though the ADA had its opponents, it ultimately created jobs for disabled Americans. Businesses had to put in a little bit to build the elevators and other accommodations, but that too created jobs.

However, the ADA also destroyed. Older towns around the country felt the impact. Workplaces on small-town Main Street didn't have room for elevators and other accommodations. Many went out of business or had to move to the strip centers outside of town. These moving businesses added to the growing suburbs, creating more opportunities for work there. But this movement was also a major factor in the decline of downtowns.

Also, for many businesses, it would now cost in excess of fifty thousand dollars extra to hire a disabled person. Employment for people with disabilities actually went down after the ADA because many businesses couldn't afford to hire them. They had to change their entire work environment—bathrooms, elevators, ramps, new computer desks, etc.—but they couldn't do so. It just became too expensive.

So Creative Destruction can bring *unintended consequences*, which occur when you don't take the time to think through what's really going to happen after you make a decision. (Unfortunately, the government never really explores the unintended consequences of its actions.) The ADA brought both opportunity and unintended consequences. Main Street suffered, but now there were opportunities to build restaurants in suburban strip malls. Many businesses struggled with the cost of implementing the changes to their buildings required by the ADA, but now people with varying degrees of ability could work virtually anywhere. This is a prime example of Creative Destruction in government law.

Creative Destruction in Technology: AI and Middle Management

We all know that technology changes rapidly. We don't even need to mention how the internet created, destroyed, and changed the world. Laptops, smartphones, and social media are other great examples of Creative Destruction at work.

The next technologies to create and destroy are algorithms and artificial intelligence (AI). People in every industry are asking, "What is AI going to do to my business?" Some are very concerned about how their jobs may be affected, even made obsolete, because of AI. Something I've been thinking about is how AI is likely to hurt the upper middle class by being a destructive force on middle management.

AI and algorithms are rapid assimilation of data. We have so much computing power we can gather, and we can read data more quickly than ever. Netflix records what you watch and then recommends movies based on what you've watched already. Google sees what you search and what you read online, then runs ads the data tells them you are likely to appreciate based on your search history. It will give you the same kind of programs, the same kind of content, and the same kind of ads to keep you watching and clicking. These are easy applications of algorithms. The computing power of AI is far greater.

Back to the middle managers. In many organizations, middle managers gather data, categorize it, and present recommendations to those above them. In these situations, the executives then do the final analysis (something AI cannot do yet) and make company decisions.

I think that AI can replace a lot of middle management. It may never be able to replace the high-end thinking of a CEO or a doctor, but for those below them in the company org chart, AI might be a destructive force that moves them out of their job.

I've heard some say that AI will never replace lawyers because the work is too technical. So, it seems that despite AI's advances, there will come a point at which the highly educated will never be replaced. I think it's also likely that people in the lower tiers of a company will also avoid replacement: drivers, factory workers, and food service will always be needed. Robotics may affect their roles in some ways, but not a lot. You're always going to need people who know how to deliver food, load trucks, cook meals, etc.

The ones who are going to suffer are the middle managers, people who are no longer needed to assimilate information so someone above them can make decisions. AI is going to have a devastating effect on lower- to middle-level people in every industry.

Globalization will play a role in the future of middle management too. Increasingly, those at the top of organizations have the ability to say, "You know, I don't need this management role on our team because I can just hire somebody from a foreign country to do this work on the cheap." Look at how many software coding jobs have already gone offshore. Some skilled labor positions will be devastated. This will lead to a greater separation of the rich and the poor.

Sawyer is not an organization built on a scaffolding of middle managers. So, I believe AI will not have as devastating an effect on Sawyer as it is likely to have on other companies. Our team is not built with information gatherers. Instead, we're staffed with more people who actually relate to customers. We're also a relatively small company, with a small leadership team and a team in manufacturing. Sawyer hires people who can analyze data and make decisions. I encourage them to do so.

Large companies and massive global brands—anybody that processes a lot of information—are the companies most likely to switch to AI for processing in the future. Those companies should ask themselves now, "Do we want our information to be processed by machines?" Sometimes yes, sometimes no. It depends upon what's at stake if you're wrong.

Creative Destruction in Cultural Norms

Imagine taking your spouse out to dinner at a nice restaurant. While you're looking over the menu, the people at the table next to yours receive plates of food that look delicious. Rather than diving into the meal, you notice one of the customers pull out his phone and take a picture of his plate. He spends a minute or two adjusting the filter on the photo and writing a post about how excited he is to eat this food. He tags the restaurant and clicks Send. Then, finally, he begins to eat.

No big deal, right? That's pretty normal for today. You may even do the same thing. This is a great example of Creative

Destruction changing cultural norms. Because this behavior is now normal, restaurants have to ensure that every dish is photogenic. You never know how big someone's social media following is, or how long your brand might be connected to a random customer's photo on the internet. What if the photo goes viral?

You may be wondering, isn't this just another example of Creative Destruction in technology? No. The technology of smartphones made it possible for everyone to take high-res, impressive-looking photos, and ubiquitous Wi-Fi created the opportunity for constant connectivity. But no one told us to take pictures of our food (behavior that previous generations would not have considered normal). Technology creates opportunity, but how we use technology is what shifts cultural norms, creating and destroying along the way.

> **Technology creates opportunity, but how we use technology is what shifts cultural norms, creating and destroying along the way.**

As we've seen, there are always unintended consequences to Creative Destruction. As customers tag restaurants in their posts, or even just use the restaurant's name, they offer the restaurant valuable marketing information. Any savvy restaurant manager will have someone monitoring a tablet equipped with all the popular social media apps. In real time they can see which customers are happy or disappointed. If they track customer posts over time, they'll undoubtedly see trends in which entrees get photographed the most along with other bits of useful information.

Sawyer regularly adjusts to shifting cultural norms. Why? Because we're always asking the most important thing you can ask as a marketer: How does my audience think? Sawyer products are most attractive to early educators and early innovators who are always seeking new information about the products they purchase. It's where we live on the bell curve. Every generation has them, but how they seek and receive information changes from one generation to the next, forcing our marketing to change with them. This change creates and destroys. Gen Z likes to use multiple devices and up to five screens, which is more than millennials do. They often mute social media videos and watch subtitles, so we responded accordingly by putting subtitles on all our videos. Gen Z also likes to have images change in videos at a faster rate, so our videos that were once tailored to millennials are now tailored to Gen Z. This shrinks (destroys) our window of conversion with millennials. If we don't get those early educators and early innovators quickly, they are probably lost because we'll have changed to meet the needs (norms) of the next generation.

There are countless more examples of Creative Destruction in cultural norms. How does your audience think? In what ways are the cultural norms shifting for your customers? These are essential questions for any marketer, entrepreneur, or business owner who wants to maximize their profits and change the world.

Look for Opportunities

I mentioned above that Creative Destruction brings both unintended consequences and opportunities. Let's take a closer look at opportunities.

In the ADA example, there was an opportunity for some people to buy old real estate in the downtowns for, as an example, twenty cents on the dollar and revitalize it. Some developers did, creating young urban professional areas. This means that some of the original building owners lost money, but it also means that some new business owners made money by creating fun places to go.

This still happens today. Savvy developers might turn old factories into condos or vacant malls into pickleball complexes. What was once an empty building can become an epicenter for entertainment. There is always an opportunity to repurpose. (The unintended consequence of the ADA was that the repurpose was forced before it was natural.)

So, there are always opportunities and they come from both sides of Creative Destruction. There are opportunities with the things that are created, and there are opportunities with the things that are destroyed. As an entrepreneur, business owner, or leader, your job is to ask, "What's life going to be like three to five years from now?" and beat everybody to the answer. This is how you make the most of the opportunities that arise from Creative Destruction. But how do you do that?

Learning to Think Ahead

One day a new team member at Sawyer, a social media marketer, asked, "How can you think ahead?"

It's a good question, but the answer isn't a secret or a superpower. Thinking ahead is a skill. Like any skill, it can be developed. Anyone can learn to think ahead with time and effort, which is why I have everyone who works for Sawyer learn and discuss these topics.

The way I develop this skill is by studying people, particularly history. I've made a conscious effort to read about every great civilization, from ancient times to recent times—Greek, Roman, Mongolian, European societies, and more. This study has shown me that humanity hasn't changed much. Human nature is to crash from within. As our societies grow wealthy, our value systems change, and then we crash. How does this apply to business? I think through questions like: How is life going to change over the next three years? How can we beat the competition? How can I figure out the changes before they do?

Something else I do is watch every news channel. I don't watch conservative or liberal news alone. I watch seven or eight different channels to see what everyone is thinking. I don't want to just know what I think. I want to know what and how they think.

The most important thing you can do to develop the skill of thinking ahead is *stop asking Google.* We have taken creative thinking out of our lives and out of our businesses. People don't think anymore. They ask Google. People ask Google questions like, "Is the answer A, B, C, or D?" But they should be asking (not Googling) questions like, "What were five reasons why we fought the Civil War?" Google will say it was to abolish slavery, which is correct, but there are lessons to learn from the other reasons. We're settling for rote answers instead of thinking. It's like settling for standardized testing instead of teaching students to write essays. People don't know how to think anymore because they aren't being taught how. So how will these future teammates at your company solve problems if they don't know how to think? We've taken thinking out of the loop.

If you want to avoid being left behind, you must learn how to think. You must learn how to assimilate information and make decisions.

The Big Idea with Creative Destruction

Creative Destruction is always there. If you put down the phone and take time to envision what life is going to be like three or five years from now, you'll start to see Creative Destruction and the opportunities it creates for your business.

Consider what the Covid-19 pandemic did for education. At every level, it's now heavily online. Before the world even knew what the coronavirus was, I worked with Messiah University in Mechanicsburg, Pennsylvania, on a digital proficiency initiative that taught their professors to use online tools for more coursework than they ever had before. Their whole curriculum eventually changed dramatically to require digital proficiency for all of their professors and students, enabling the students to be better prepared for working at places like Sawyer. I worked with Messiah in this way because, as a businessman, I was frustrated that I wasn't getting employees with the technical qualities I wanted. And as a philanthropist, I wanted to invest in a school that I believe in (and where my daughter Gwen played basketball and our other daughter, Bethany, studied special needs education). I also saw how the internet was inevitably going to change education. When the pandemic finally hit the US, Messiah University was ready.

Look at the workforce after Covid. It seems that nobody wants to go to work anymore. They want to work from home. No one knew the pandemic was coming, but as soon as it came, those who are practiced at thinking ahead could figure out what might happen to their workforce. That was the time to get out of corporate real estate because nobody was going to go back to the office for a couple of years. Look at the occupancy rates in New

York City. Those who own large corporate buildings, and who weren't thinking ahead, are facing some hard questions about what to do with their corporate space.[12]

Or start thinking about things closer to home. Sit down with your spouse and ask: What do you think it is going to be like three years from now? What kind of cars will we drive? What school will our kids go to? What is going to change at that school? Put down your phone and think through things like that.

Unless you work in tech, you probably won't be able to predict how technology will change your family. And no one can accurately predict political changes right now. But something you can count on is that changes are coming. You can take time to envision what's coming, or not. Thinking ahead is a skill you can develop. I believe people know how to do it. They just don't.

People often say I'm a "visionary." I appreciate the compliment, but I'm not a visionary. I'm just thinking through Creative Destruction.

Ruined for Good: How The Bucket Ministry Began

Picture yourself drinking dirty river water every day. The same river that cows, dogs, and other animals from the nearby community drink from . . . and relieve themselves in. The same river that clothes, dishes, and other household items are washed in. A river that includes runoff from nearby roads and motorboats, as well as trash from the next community upstream.

---

12 Phillip Pilkington, "Work from home and empty offices leading to 'doom loop' for NYC: study," *New York Post*, updated June 8, 2023, https://nypost.com/2023/06/08/work-from-home-and-empty-offices-leading-to-doom-loop-for-nyc/.

To many of us in the Western world, a scene like this only exists on the pages of *National Geographic*. Even poor people wouldn't actually drink water from a river that contaminated—would they?

In 2012, my friend Chris Beth visited the Amazon River and its surrounding area. He was on a mission trip with his teenage daughter and their church. In his own words, he wasn't serious about his faith or doing charitable work at that time in his life. He was only on that trip "to be her dad. I just wanted to make sure she came home."

After landing in Manaus, Brazil, they traveled eighteen hours by open-air riverboat down the Amazon River, where they would stop at a number of small villages. During the trip, Chris spent time with a family in their house, which was built on the banks of the Amazon. This wasn't a gilded riverside cottage like you'd see in a posh neighborhood along the Mississippi. This house was a ramshackle structure perched near moldering docks in one of the poorest regions of the world. After spending a few hours with the family who lived there, Chris was hot and clearly sweating.

"Would you like a drink of water?" his hostess asked through his interpreter and guide. Chris said yes and then watched as this longtime resident of the Amazon grabbed two drinking glasses, walked out on a dock, and dipped the glasses directly into the river. She returned and gave one to Chris and one to his guide. Chris was speechless. *This was honestly the water that she and her family drank every day?* In Chris's words, "That experience ruined me."

Suddenly and unexpectedly, Chris had a new life mission.

"I came back to the US with this burden on my heart to help them," Chris told me. "But what would it mean to help these people? I had no idea. I just kept thinking about seeing them drink dirty water from a river and I didn't know what to do about it."

Chris started to learn some staggering statistics about the global water crisis like those we discussed in the last chapter. More than eight hundred thousand people die every year because of health complications related to drinking unsafe water, and he had seen it up close. The family he'd spent that afternoon with had no idea how bad their water was. Or, if they did know, it didn't matter because they had no other recourse. He had the sad realization that "the water I wash my car with is cleaner than what most people have access to."

Chris knew he had to do something. He soon started researching water wells and water filters. He spoke with a medical doctor who had traveled with them and learned that *every person* treated during their trip desperately needed clean water. "They all have symptoms of waterborne disease," the doctor told him. "*They think that diarrhea is normal.*"

Chris doubled down on his research into water filters versus digging wells. He reviewed hundreds of options and eventually settled on filters as the most economical and long-lasting. Chris later settled on Sawyer PointONE Hollow-Fiber Membrane Filters as the most effective for his new mission. Here is how he tells the story:

> My wife and I were at REI in Dallas. I was looking at water filters and found this Sawyer water filter. The package made this ridiculous claim that it lasted for a million gallons and that it took out basically everything that I was researching was a problem. So,

I bought two bucket system filters. I went home, got on the internet, and started reading the lab results of the Sawyer water filters. I thought, my goodness, this thing is portable! It's simple to run, you don't need to be an engineer, and it's long-lasting. It was all the things that I needed in the Amazon basin where water rises and falls so much that people often have to move their homes. I knew I could teach a six-year-old or a ninety-six-year-old how to clean the thing.

To finalize his decision to use a Sawyer filter over all the other filters and clean water solutions he'd been researching, Chris put the filter through the ultimate test.

"I told my wife, 'Hey, we're going to conduct an experiment and drink water out of Lake Ray Hubbard for the next week.'" Though his wife was skeptical at first—she's a registered nurse and fully understood the danger of having the family drink lake water for a week—she reviewed the lab tests and then she and their children joined in the experiment.

Chris said that "by the end of the week, none of us could tell the difference between lake water coming through the Sawyer filter and a bottle of Ozarka, as long as both the waters were cold. *And nobody got sick*! So, the experiment passed. This was what we would use to help the people we met in the Amazon."

The Bucket Ministry (TBM) was born not long after. Chris, who had been a business consultant for thirty-five years at that point, eventually left his work and now runs TBM full-time. Chris and his team travel all over the world distributing Sawyer International Bucket Systems, training people on how to use and clean them, and then they conduct multiple follow-up visits weeks and months afterward in which they record data on their improving physical and spiritual health.

In his own words: "Since my trip in 2012, TBM has served over *one million* people with hope. Hope that tomorrow they will not have to drink unclean water. Hope that their children will not be sick anymore from drinking from a mud puddle. Hope that they can hear about a friend that will never leave them, that they can put their trust and lives in."

You're going to read more about TBM throughout this book. They've become strategic partners with Sawyer in fighting the global water crisis. Chris's big vision to take clean water to the poorest areas of the world and to follow up every donated filter with training, multiple return visits, and a message of faith inspires me.

In this chapter, we've talked about Creative Destruction, the process by which industries destroy and create themselves from within, through innovative developments, *often achieved by entrepreneurs introducing something revolutionary*. We've said that Creative Destruction is an essential fact of capitalism and economic growth. Chris's story demonstrates a different kind of Creative Destruction. When he was given a glass of dirty water to drink by a humble, unassuming family, something was destroyed inside of him. But out of that, something new was created too, an innovative way to bring access to clean water to anyone in need.

Can you imagine drinking a glass of dirty river water? Chris couldn't either.

Now no one has to.

Chapter Three
Financing the Business

I love talking to entrepreneurs. They are passionate people who typically desire to change the world and disrupt the status quo. I can identify with that. There are three pieces of advice I often share when I'm talking with entrepreneurs, especially when it comes to financing their businesses.

First, *find out all the reasons why you won't be successful.* Even if you've invented a new mouse trap, let rejection teach you. The advice you get in a rejection will help you see the holes in your idea that you can't see. Being rejected can reveal the pitfalls that may be ahead for you.

Shark Tank is a great example of this. Everybody on that show thinks they have the new sliced bread. Yet only 40 percent of them actually get the deal. The other 60 percent get thrown out. So, before you face the sharks, find out all the reasons why you won't be successful.

The second piece of advice, a lesson I learned at the Northwestern Kellogg School of Management,[13] was that if you're looking for finance, *make sure you get rejected three times.* Every entrepreneur needs to get more than one person's opinion. Not every shark thinks the same way.

It's helpful to remember that someone who rejects your idea may not know what they're talking about. They may not even know the industry. So, try to get qualified people. Find people who know something about something and who will tell you the risks in your idea. Don't just share your idea with Aunt Susie and think that is enough. Find people who have achieved success, even if it's success in a different area than you. Ask each of them to tell you why you may not succeed. Then think about how you can weave your way around the obstacles they identify to find just the right entry point and carve out your niche.

This leads to a third piece of advice for entrepreneurs: *rejection doesn't mean you stop, but it might mean you need to make adjustments*. You hear things like this all the time on *Shark Tank*: "Forget retail. Stay online. Pivot." If you truly have something good, there's a niche for it somewhere. But you've got to make sure you find that niche and stay in it.

In the very beginning of Sawyer Products, we went to all the grocery stores with the Extractor™ Pump Kit, a product for removing venom from a bee sting or snake bite. Nobody wanted it. I realized, OK, grocery stores are not going to be a channel of distribution for us. But then we made sales calls to drugstores to see if we could talk them into the Extractor™ Pump Kit, as

---

13 The Northwestern Kellogg School of Management is in Evanston, Illinois, and is consistently ranked as one of the top business schools in the country.

this made sense in a drugstore. Eventually, we ended up selling in stores that served campers and hikers. We found our niche. To this day, grocery stores and drugstores are not for us. We had to pivot and work to find our niche.

Free Money

Every new business needs capital. It may take passion to start a new venture, but it takes capital to actually turn the lights on and sustain the organization. But capital is expensive. How do you get it? How can you afford it?

The lowest cost of capital you'll ever get is your accounts payable to your vendors. This may seem counterintuitive, but think about it. If you borrow money from the bank, you're going to pay interest. If you borrow money from venture capital, you're going to pay a huge price in equity. But if you borrow money by not paying your bills, and if you have a vendor who understands that you're worth the risk—someone who will extend dating from 30 to 90 to 120 days—you can't get cheaper money than that. But to make it worth their while, you need to stay in their loyal base.

> **The lowest cost of capital you'll ever get is your accounts payable to your vendors.**

The math on the vendor side is a no-brainer. They pay interest on their cost, which is a small fraction of the profit they can get from a good, loyal customer. This is why I call it "free money." Because from your perspective, you can start your company without a lot of capital.

It starts by picking the right vendors. It needs to be worth more to them to continue selling to you than to collect the money right away. Stay loyal to them. Keep purchasing your supplies from them because their credit is what's going to let you build your company. (We will talk more about how to be in the loyal base in Chapter Seven, "The Circle of Customers.") Other money is expensive. Venture capital will kill you. Your supplier will pay a lower interest rate and it is only on their cost, not your cost. The little interest they pay—.07 times $5.00 divided by four (three months of 7 percent interest)—comes to only costing them $.09 to protect a $4.91 profit. That is a no-brainer for them if they trust you.

When Mark Zuckerberg started Facebook, he had to use venture capital. He was raising fifty to one hundred million dollars. But let's say you're starting a local restaurant. You might only need one hundred thousand dollars. If you get fifty thousand of it in credit for free from your vendors, then you only need to pay interest on the other fifty thousand. So, it depends on what you're starting and how big you are (or wish to become).

What Businesses Should Avoid Doing

Don't give up stock. If you're short on capital, you may be tempted to do so. Instead, keep control of your company and bring your money in as loans from an investor rather than from equity. Why? Because loans are the best way for your company and for the investor to lower the combined tax burden. Dividends paid on equity are taxed twice: first to the corporation for its profit and then again to the stockholder on the dividend. The interest on loans is tax-deductible to the corporation. The lender pays taxes on the interest received, so the IRS only collects taxes once (from the lender), while the corporation gets a deduction. With stock, the corporation pays taxes on the profits needed to support a dividend, and the owner pays taxes on the dividend and on any capital gains when they sell the stock. The difference is being taxed once versus being taxed twice and perhaps three times. Thus, loans are a much lower cost to finance a company from the lender's point of view, therefore making it easier to raise funds.

Also, if you get somebody to agree to a loan, then you haven't given up control like you would if they put their money in equity. Of course, it's wise to allow a person who loans a large amount of money to have some say about what's going on, whether it's equity or not. But technically speaking, loans don't force you to give up control.

Lastly, be ready to experience a paradigm shift when you enter a new industry. One of my biggest challenges in the early days of Sawyer was that I didn't adjust from where I had been to where I was going as an entrepreneur. I left big corporations that spent large sums of advertising money the way big corporations do. I realized that with much smaller promotional budgets I needed to focus on what I could do through guerilla marketing. So, you need to know your paradigm shift. Are you trained properly, or can you get trained properly, to be successful in your new venture? It might be modified skill sets or just thinking differently.

Lastly, don't go public. Going public with your business isn't the worst thing in the world. It may even be what's best for you at a certain time. But that's not where I'm at. I don't like going public because you can't do your philanthropic work.

A Fourth Piece of Advice for NGOs

Speaking of philanthropy work, this chapter began with three pieces of advice for entrepreneurs, but here's a fourth one just for NGOs. It has to do with *passion*.

Passion is what drives most entrepreneurs, including those who start nonprofits. I think that's great. Follow your passions and be passionate about what you pursue. But know that *passion can get in the way of realistically accessing what issues may lie ahead.*

This can be a problem for entrepreneurs entering the market, but it can be especially problematic for nonprofits. Nonprofits are almost always passion-driven. They have a vision and a passion and that's what they sell.

The problem is that they are almost always selling an emotional experience, and they're trying to sell it to investors. You can get a few investors to have an emotional experience with you. Small investors may want to put a single bucket filter out there or send meals to somebody overseas. That person can be won with passion.

But as soon as you want to go for the big bucks, you have to be able to explain the return on investment (ROI). If an investor has a million dollars ready to donate, they will most certainly want to donate it to an organization that will provide the biggest bang for the buck. Because chances are, if they have a million dollars, they also run a successful business and think like that. But there are many entrepreneurial NGOs who only operate based on their passion, and they're not ready with ROI information for big investors.

So, we've empowered the charities we work with to provide metrics and demonstrate the ROI of each investment. Our primary method for gathering this data is through geographic information system (GIS) tracking. Through a unique barcode or QR code on each water filter, we can gather data and assess the impact of the water filter. We can learn how many people are no longer getting sick in that household or community, how much money the family is saving by no longer having to purchase water (money they can then spend on other important needs), and, if we're working with a faith-based NGO, how many people have heard a presentation of the gospel.

Some real-life examples of data we've gathered through GIS tracking are:

1. 95 percent of waterborne diseases are gone within two weeks.
2. Household savings between 12 percent and 30 percent from not having to buy water. That's money that can be used to buy other essential needs.
3. Many, many lives of young children are saved.
4. A huge reduction in the use of fossil fuels needed to boil water.
5. Millions of trees are not needed for fuel, which reduces deforestation.
6. Improved mental capacity of people who are no longer dulled by dehydration.
7. Improved happiness and family cohesiveness.

And much more.

Calculating Environmental Impact

Giving someone access to clean water does more than meet their immediate need for safe water. It also makes a positive impact on the environment. In many parts of the world, people boil water daily in order to have clean water for drinking and cooking. This means they are constantly burning wood, or, in some cases, fossil fuels. A Sawyer water filter makes the boiling of water and the burning of wood unnecessary.

The engineering team at Sawyer has come up with a way for us to estimate how much wood is saved when someone has access to a filter.

Variables:
- Water temp at the start
- Stove versus open fire efficiency (40 percent vs. 20 percent)
- Hardness of the wood
- Fossil fuel option

Assumptions:
- Four different filter options serving one to one hundred people
- Each filter lasts ten years (many have proven to last longer)
- Average of two gallons per person per day

Equals:
- 100 to 400 trees per person for ten years or equivalent fossil fuel
- 500 to 2,000 trees for a family of five for ten years or equivalent fossil fuel
- 2,000 to 8,000 trees for a group of twenty per filter (done frequently) for ten years or equivalent fossil fuels.

Therefore, we are confident that, with over a million filters in use around the world, we are *saving over two hundred million trees per year*, or equivalent fossil fuel, as of year-end 2023. This number increases each year as more filters are placed in homes, orphanages, schools, and more.

Remember Chris Beth and his experience in the Amazon that led to The Bucket Ministry from the last chapter? TBM is a great example of a nonprofit organization that has learned the value of tracking ROI for its donors. Chris and his team, along with a data-collecting and analyzing company called Sparrow, have developed a proprietary GIS software called Mission Mapping. Through follow-up visits with indigenous teams, TBM tracks the improving physical and spiritual health of everyone who receives a bucket filter system from them. At each visit, they scan the code on the filter which opens a survey for collecting information about the family's physical and spiritual health. Updated photos of the recipients are also taken. Each family is visited three times within the first several months of receiving a water filter. This process produces a report card for the donors who can view the information online.[14] TBM has recorded incredible stories of improved health and quality of life through their Mission Mapping software. Here are just three real-life examples of ROI from TBM's charitable work in Kibera, Kenya, all of it captured by the indigenous team they work with:

> *Eunice's husband had stomach problems before receiving the bucket filter. Their baby was also being*

---

14 www.thebucketministry.org/recipient-mapping/

troubled with skin rashes. Any time [the husband] drank any water that was not filtered he would have diarrhea. After receiving the filter Eunice started washing her baby with filtered water and the husband started drinking filtered water. Since then, the baby's skin rashes have disappeared and the husband no longer has stomach problems.

Lindah had rashes all over her face when she came for the bucket filter. She heard during the filter demonstration that if she used the filtered water the rashes would disappear. And true to that word, it happened to her.

The diarrhea case was rampant among the family members. They often visited the medical centre for attention and treatment. But after receiving the bucket filter, the issue stopped, which is evident by the gladness on their faces, their testimonials, and attending their daily chores without worries.

Imagine being a donor and receiving real-time, real-life information *like that* on a regular basis. The Bucket Ministry has ROI down to a science. Their donors can visit the Mission Mapping website at any time and see where in the world the filters are located and read a real-time report card about the recipients' improved health. But I've met too many others running charities who don't even think about using technology like this. They're not thinking about using metrics. They just show you a picture of the kid you're investing in. So, what about the donor who gives a million dollars? What are you going to do, send her a million pictures? She is a businessperson and wants a business ROI analysis.

Sometimes I've been in discussion about these things with the president or director of an NGO and they'll balk at the increased cost that ROI analysis entails. "I can't spend that," they'll say. "That's another three bucks a kid," or whatever the additional cost may be. I understand that initial reaction, but once you start demonstrating ROI effectively, you're going to raise another thirty bucks for those three bucks you spent. The big donors will show up when you give them the metrics.

Why We Work Hard on Sawyer's Finances: The Water Crisis in Liberia

Liberia is a small country on the western edge of Africa. It's about the size of Pennsylvania or Louisiana (43,000 square miles), with 350 miles of shoreline on the Atlantic Ocean. More than five million people are native to Liberia. Until November 2020, most of the population did not have access to clean water.

In 2008 a young pastor from Washington DC, Todd Phillips, set an audacious goal: to bring clean water to every person in Liberia by 2020. He began a nonprofit organization called The Last Well. Here is how this ministry describes itself: "The vision to eliminate water scarcity in Liberia, West Africa by the year 2020 was birthed in 2008 by young Christian adults at a church in Washington D.C. led by Todd Phillips. They were all inspired by the movie *Amazing Grace* that chronicled the life of William Wilberforce who is credited with the historic feat of ending the slave trade in England. Together, they set out to make their own history and rallied around the cause of providing a nation access to safe drinking water."[15]

The Last Well aimed to dig new wells across Liberia. The project was estimated to cost $31 million over twelve years. But if The Last Well were to succeed, Liberia would become the first developing nation with border-to-border basic access to clean water. I didn't know Todd Phillips when he began this work in 2008, but I admire his thinking. He strikes me as someone who has a very big God.

"Our babies are dying!"

Liberia suffered an Ebola crisis in 2015. The Last Well had been hard at work for seven years at that point, though the goal of border-to-border access to clean water hadn't been met. The team at Sawyer decided to send our International Director, Darrel Larson, to Liberia that year. We sent Darrel for a few reasons.

First, he was there to visit with people who already had filters and to gather data about what impact the filters might be making in people's lives. Darrel partnered with Calvin University to perform a formal research project about the effects of using a water filter in this area. They used an unbiased survey to gather data on various subjects, like:

---

15 "About Us," The Last Well, accessed January 17, 2024, https://thelastwell.org/about/.

- If the filters were working properly
- If not, then diagnosing what went wrong
- The number of days children had to miss school due to illness since they started using the water filter
- How often the adults in each household had to miss work due to diarrhea (or other waterborne illness) since they started using the water filter
- How often they had to purchase clean water and what the "purchased water savings" are
- The number of medical visits they've had to schedule since they began using the water filter
- As well as other similar subjects

Darrel was also there to distribute more filters through a team of Liberian nationals. This means Darrel led multiple trainings on how to properly install, clean, and otherwise use the Sawyer water filters. We've learned that—if we want to create lasting change—it is critical to build capacity into local people rather than just hand them a filter.

Another reason Darrel was there was to help The Last Well. Todd Phillips had asked Sawyer to partner with The Last Well in order to help complete their mission of border-to-border clean water for Liberia by 2020. Some villages were so remote that it was impossible for wells to be dug. Plus, the cost of digging a well versus distributing a Sawyer water filter is significant. A new well in Liberia cost roughly $3,000 at that time. The cost per beneficiary of getting a water filter was four times cheaper than digging a well. It's also much easier and less costly to maintain and replace handheld water filters over the years than wells.

On his trip, Darrel visited Sumah Town, a large village in Bong County (north-central Liberia), where a handful of families were piloting Sawyer water filters. He prepared to do a follow-up visit and collect data on how the filter had affected their lives. Word got out about Darrel's visit, and he was greeted by a large group of people from the village when he arrived, though at first not all of them looked friendly.

"When we first drove up," Darrel says, "there were guys playing soccer in a field nearby. A bunch of them had machetes. As soon as they saw us, they quit the soccer and started walking towards us—with their machetes! I didn't know what was going on. I just remember thinking, what is about to happen?"

As intimidating as that was, the men were simply carrying their machetes—which they used for work—with them.

"They were there to greet us and welcome us to the village! They were so happy we were there," Darrel said.

This entourage of machete-wielding people quickly led Darrel and his team of Liberian trainers to an influential woman in their village. She was young, probably not older than twenty-five, and holding a baby wearing a dirty T-shirt.

"You have to bring these!" she said immediately and emphatically, indicating the filters. "I'm going to take you and show you where I've got to get water every day."

With the baby still in her arms, she led Darrel and the others down toward a large pond filled with cloudy water the color of milky coffee. Mosquitos were everywhere skimming the water, and there was a thick layer of muck along the pond's edge. Sticks and debris floated in the water, and animals nearby no doubt drank from and relieved themselves in the pond or close to it. The woman pointed to the water and then to a filter.

"You have to bring me these! You *have* to! This water is killing our babies."

Darrel would tell me later, "This lady had lasers in her eyes."

"Our babies are dying!" she yelled through tears, agitating the baby on her hip who also began to cry. "Our babies are dying!"

In Liberia, it's very common to ask this tragic question: "How many babies have you birthed and how many are still living?" It's baffling and heartbreaking to imagine what it must be like to live in a culture where the death of one's children is so commonplace. Think of the emotional, spiritual, and psychological toll the death of a child takes.

But that's exactly where someone from Sawyer needed to be. I've heard Darrel tell this story many times. He says, "The beauty of that story is that *we were* going to be there. We'd already donated some filters to that village and were able to clearly see their impact based on the data we were gathering. Soon after that encounter with the woman, our team of Liberian trainers began their work and in a short time the whole village had access to clean water."

"When you see and hear the visceral plea of a mother with a baby in her hand you can't unsee it," Darrel says. How can we not do *something*?

The residents of Sumah Town gathered around their water source.

Build Capacity in People

In 2015 Darrel began training thirty Liberians who had been brought together from various other nonprofits by The Last Well. (Just getting all the nonprofits to work together was a miracle and could be the subject of another book!) Three trainers rose to the top of the group—Elijah Harlie, Sam Tablo, and Othello Johnson. These three were orators and natural leaders. They were more educated than many of the others and became important trainers whom The Last Well continued using to train more people around the country. About two hundred Liberians were trained over the next few years through Darrel's work with The Last Well and local community leaders like Elijah, Sam, and Othello.

This is what it looks like to build capacity within local people. Our vision is *not* to send teams of Sawyer people around the world. Instead, we invest in community leaders who are already there. Projects are more sustainable that way. We teach them how to use the filters and the best practices for sustainability (like doing their own follow-up visits), as well as behavior changes (like washing hands and avoiding the pollution of water sources with human and animal waste). Then they pass that information along from village to village. "A big part of my job," Darrel says, "is capacity-building, passing along best practices, and teaching the value of data."

This training is now available by phone anywhere in the world. A QR code on each filter connects users to our website and to animation videos about installing and maintaining the filter, as well as the WASH principle (water, sanitation, and hygiene recommendations) in local languages and dialects.

We plan a series of follow-up visits to every family who receives a water filter. We visually inspect the filters and ensure that they know how to clean them every day. We monitor the diarrhea rates and research subjects like those listed above.

When faced with needs as great as those represented in Liberia—where mothers literally cry out for help so their babies won't die—it's tempting to think, what difference could we possibly make? This chapter is about financing your business. With your finances in order, imagine the difference your company might make in a place where there is tremendous need. It's worth asking again, how big is your God?

Chapter Four

Managing the Business

The first handheld calculator was invented by Texas Instruments in 1967 and hit the commercial market in 1970. Though people had been using abacuses for as far back as recorded history goes, the handheld calculator was a game changer. People began to do precise mathematical computations with a machine that fit in their pockets. What an innovation![16]

With all due respect to the good folks at Texas Instruments, I'd like to tell you to *stop using your calculator*. Put away your phone. Close the app on your computer. The more you rely on a calculator to do your thinking for you, the less you'll understand how numbers work and your business or nonprofit will suffer for it. Besides, sometimes you don't need to know the exact numbers in order to make a decision, you just need to know what range you're in.

---

16 Anuli Akanegbu and Ricky Ribeiro, "The History of Calculators: Evolution of the Calculator (Timeline)," November 20, 2012, https://edtechmagazine.com/k12/article/2012/11/calculating-firsts-visual-history-calculators.

In this chapter, we're going to be talking about a concept that is fundamental to strategic thinking—understanding the relationship between numerators and denominators. It's both simple and complicated. I call it *Math Trap*. If you understand it, you can make good business decisions more quickly and come up with correct strategies without knowing all the details. It's the secret sauce to maximizing your profits, saving money, and then using that money to change the world.

It's just math.

Why We Didn't Take On OFF!®

In 1990 Sawyer won a significant federal contract to produce sunblock (now called sunscreens) and insect repellents for troops fighting in Operation Desert Shield. (I'll tell you more of the incredible story of winning this contract in a later chapter.) By 1991 we acquired Coulston, a company that developed a consumer-grade, permethrin-based insect repellent. That same year we manufactured Controlled Release Insect Repellent Lotions and introduced them to the consumer market as a high-end alternative insect repellent. Though we were still a young company at that time, about a decade old, we were suddenly entering a consumer market that clearly had "big dogs" who owned most of the market share. Figuring out how to sell our repellent was going to be a challenge.

Eighty to ninety percent of the insect repellent market was tied up with two companies. SC Johnson® (which owns OFF!®) had probably 50 percent of the market share and Spectrum® (which owns Cutter® and Repel®) had the other 30 percent or so. I knew two things right away:

1. It would be stupid to take on the big brands. Their power is more in their brand strength than their products, and I didn't want to do a copycat product anyway. Why produce something that somebody else was already making?
2. Oftentimes, the number three brand in market share is very profitable. So, it really didn't matter if Sawyer ended up with 2 percent, 4 percent, or 8 percent of the market. Our strategy would remain the same.

How did I know we could be successful without taking on the industry leader? How did I know that being third or fourth in the market would be OK, even profitable? Because of Math Trap, the relationship between the numerator and the denominator. It's easiest to explain with something you may be familiar with already—baseball cards.

Batting Averages and the Brooklyn Dodgers

When I was a wee little tyke I would go to my grandpa's house next door, sit on the floor, and listen to baseball games on the radio with him. He was always listening to the Brooklyn Dodgers. I became a fan of the "boys of summer" because that's who Grandpa listened to. I knew all the players of the time and was even given (and still have) a 1957 Brooklyn Dodgers yearbook. I continued to follow the Dodgers after they moved to LA before the 1958 season. Through the '60s I was wowed by players like Sandy Koufax and Duke Snider and in the '70s by the four men who made up what is often considered the best infield in baseball history: Steve Garvey, Davey Lopes, Ron Cey, and Bill Russell.

As I grew up, I collected baseball cards. On the back of most baseball cards is a chart filled with the player's stats—their numbers. One of the most important stats of the day was a player's batting average. This number was used to determine how good of a hitter he was. It represented how likely he might be to get a hit during each at bat. A player's batting average is determined by dividing a player's hits by his total at-bats (excluding walks and sacrifices) for a number between zero and 1.000. So, every hit matters . . . or does it?

Let's say Dodger's slugger Duke Snider had ten at-bats and had four hits. Four divided by ten—Duke's batting .400. Let's say in the next game Duke goes two-for-two (two hits in two at-bats). Now he's six-for-twelve across the two games. Duke's batting .500. His average moved from .400 to .500 with just two hits.

Now let's say Duke has had five hundred at-bats and two hundred hits. He's still batting .400. The next day Duke goes two for two again. This time Duke's two hits moved his batting average a whopping .003 points for a total of .403 (202 hits over 502 at-bats). In one case Duke added one hundred points. In the other, he only added three.

This understanding between numerators and denominators is how I knew that Sawyer could enter the insect repellent market without taking on the big dogs and still be profitable. Math Trap helped me quickly make the decision to enter a field dominated by big brands with confidence.

Like a player with five hundred at-bats, OFF!® and Cutter® would have to fight for every little percentage point gain in the market, while a small company like Sawyer could make dramatic increases in profit with our relatively small share, just like a player who jumps .100 points with just two hits in a few at-bats. I was aiming to position our topical and clothing repellents as high-performance alternatives. Sawyer didn't need to have the largest piece of the pie in order to make this work.

With niche marketing, the number three and four in any market can make a lot of money because they can put all of their resources into one segment of the market. That is Math Trap—trapping the industry by knowing relatively where you are within it. It really doesn't matter if your business has 5, 8, or 12 percent of the market. Your whole strategy, because you are number three or four, is totally different than the strategies of one or two. Let the big companies spend time and money determining if they are 18.6 percent of the market or 21.4 percent. Your strategy is not going to change.

The question becomes, how do you find your niche?

Determining Our Unique Selling Position

Not only did I want to avoid producing a copycat product, but Sawyer also did not have the ad budget of a big corporation. It wouldn't have been wise to challenge OFF!®, and we couldn't have done it if we wanted to, not with ads. So, it was imperative for us to find a niche and work around them. We had to produce something different than what they offered and find our own unique place in the market. After a few years, we eventually brought out picaridin insect repellent. Picaridin is the high-end of insect repellent. It's easier on your skin, easier on the equipment, and it lasts longer.

We also avoided the channels of distribution and the formulas of the big corporations. We didn't bring out 10 percent

DEET formula for the moms in a white bottle like they did. Sawyer repellent had a Controlled Release formula, which we position as better. Ironically, it's also the first choice for the military because they use repellents frequently, so it needs to be gentle on the skin while still being very effective. We didn't give customers 30 percent and 40 percent DEET. We just couldn't go there. That would be a copycat product and we had no interest in that.

This goes back to something we discussed in Chapter One, understanding where you are on the bell curve. Those interested in Sawyer repellents are on the far end. We're often purchased by early educators and early innovators. While OFF!® and Cutter® run ads during a baseball game, our customers are learning about us on social media. They're listening to influencers and well-known hikers, campers, hunters, and others talk about how effective our product is in the real world. We treasure these authentic endorsements. We don't pay anybody and we don't want to rely on actors and actresses to say our stuff is good. We look to online influencers to praise our products because the products are truly better, not because they were paid. Sawyer's goal is to always move the ball forward in product technology—to offer something better that the end consumer needs.

This niche market is also listening to our story. Social media is far better than TV ads for telling stories. Being a social media brand has given us new opportunities to tell stories about impoverished people around the world and raise money through the Sawyer Foundation. Sawyer makes major investments in life-changing water projects in developing countries. Social media influencers help us tell that story.

We also did a few new things on packaging to disrupt our market. We blasted out the picaridin and permethrin names on our packaging. These are the products that The Centers for Disease Control and Prevention (CDC) and others recommend so it is usually our brand products they show as examples. Priceless publicity. But these are still small niches so the major brands are not yet truly interested. Other products listed picaridin down in the fine print. Well, after our success they're starting to put picaridin up where you can see it, but it is still a small niche. Even the big brands will sell picaridin and let you know it's picaridin, but they don't really push it because it's so much more expensive.

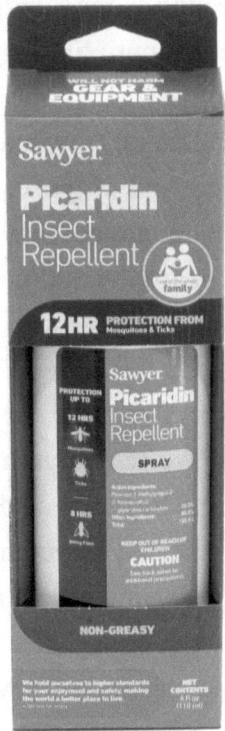

An example of Sawyer Insect Repellent with "Picaridin" featured prominently.

How Math Trap Can Save You Money

I joined Weed Eater as a marketing manager in 1982. It was only their eleventh year. The business was still going crazy. I quickly learned that there were three variables that mattered:

1. How long the product you made would last.
2. The likelihood that consumers would replace it when it broke (which was pretty high for Weed Eater at the time because consumers were not going to go back to clipping grass by hand).
3. The penetration into the household—how many you have sold. There are roughly one hundred million households in the US. That is approximately sixty million homes with some kind of lawn, and only a portion of those will own their own trimmers. How many new households are formed each year? And of those, how many will want a trimmer? How many already have a trimmer? And then how many new people would come in, and how many replacements would come in? So, it's just math.

After joining the team, I realized they had their projections going in a straight line. "We're just going to keep growing and growing" was the attitude. They projected 15 percent growth that year. But my research indicated something different. I believed they'd shifted into the decreasing rate of increase on the product life cycle curves and instead projected something like 7 percent growth. Based on the percentage of new households, the percentage of failures, and the percentage of replacements, I laid out my rationale. "We put it together and you can't grow 15 percent," I said to my supervisor. "There's no market left." There were not enough new places to go. So, we were only going to have replacement sales and a lower number of new sales.

Not everyone on the team agreed, but I was eventually invited to share my thoughts with the powers that be. While their numbers were fairly reasonable, they were still projecting higher growth than they should've expected. That meant the company would be spending a lot on manufacturing inventory that, if I was right, would gather dust in a warehouse.

We continued to discuss the life cycle curves and they eventually realized that they had run out of new households to buy their trimmers. There were still some households buying the new time trimmers, but not as many as they thought. They didn't realize the market had been saturated. And as much as they may have wanted to, they couldn't change the life cycle curve. The curve was going to bend, whether it was my numbers or their numbers. That's the Math Trap conclusion. The money coming in was going to be less no matter which number they picked. The unit sales were going to be less than their original projections no matter what assumptions we reasonably made. You can't keep selling if there's no market left.

I call it making projections by looking in the rearview mirror when companies make their projections only by considering what they did last year or over the last few years. Those numbers are helpful, but things change so that can't be your only point of reference.

Eventually, the president bought in. He directed the production lines to produce a much lower number of units and we hit our new projections on one-tenth of 1 percent! It was incredible. This saved Weed Eater from manufacturing a lot of excess inventory. It also helped the company avoid a scenario during the next year when they would've had to sell off old inventory, ultimately making them less money.

They understood that the success of Weed Eater had given them a huge denominator and that whether we sold 15 percent more or 7 percent more the change to the numerator wouldn't be significant enough to change the overall "batting average" on the bottom line. However, by planning for 7 percent growth, we could save millions of dollars in production and inventory costs.

Let's look at another example. This time we'll move out of the manufacturer's office and into retail.

Say you have a plumbing supply business and carry $50,000 worth of inventory. Meanwhile, your competitor carries $100,000 in inventory. If you and your competitor do the same amount of business, who is going to make more money? You will because you've turned more of your inventory. With the profit, you could open up a second shop with another $50,000 of inventory. The other guy can't because he's still got so much tied up in his inventory. You could have two shops at $50,000 each. You can do a lot more with your money than he can.

That's what Walmart did. By managing the denominator more than the numerator, they learned how to basically have a free store. They turned inventory so fast that there was less investment tied up in the products in the stores. They did this by only having to invest in the building and infrastructure. By turning the inventory so fast—selling it before having to pay their vendors—the inventory in the store requires practically no investment dollars. While their competitors had to invest in both the stores and the inventory, Walmart was able to add stores and grow sales faster than the others. The lower denominator also yielded higher ROIs. They knew it was more important to reduce their investment in their building than it was to sell more products out of that building. They knew that you could only sell so much. Maybe you can grow sales a little here and there, maybe 3 or 4 percent year over year, and that's wonderful, but if you cut your denominator in half then you double your ROI. They did this by saving money on their inventory investment. This strategy allowed them to block out most of their competitors. Small businesses and entrepreneurs need to think differently than big corporations. If you currently work for a big corporation and you want to start your own business, reprogram yourself.

People are prone to let the numbers get in the way. They focus too much on them in specific terms rather than thinking about how they work together. Large corporations might spend infinite amounts of time collecting data so they can determine if they own 4.5 percent or 4.7 percent of the market. Who cares? When your denominator is that big, those percentage points aren't going to change the way you sell cereal or SUVs or whatever your business is.

There's definitely a place for complex math like regression analysis, amortization, and other concepts, especially in the world of finance and investing. But sometimes in marketing the simple math is all you need.

Reverse Math Trap

Sometimes you need to know when you don't have a chance anymore—when something just isn't worth it.

In 2018 the Ford Motor Company announced that it would stop producing cars other than the Ford Mustang.[17] The Taurus, the Fusion, and the Fiesta would all be discontinued. They weren't worth it to Ford anymore. They would instead only manufacture trucks, SUVs, and crossover-utility vehicles. They'd lost too much market share and knew there was no way to get it back. So, to heck with it. SUVs are basically truck frames and that market was booming. Newer brands focused their resources and money on the large sedan market segment and pushed Ford out. Oh well. Ford then focused on the profitable markets where they do well and can defend their share.

That's the reverse Math Trap. That's knowing when a segment has become unprofitable and not worth it to compete. I bet it didn't take much thinking at the very, very top to figure that out, while down below all the accountants, product managers, and plant managers were fighting like crazy to keep their little niches going. Math Trap thinking prevents you from getting bogged down by the details from accountants and the warring plant managers so you can see the range you're in and make a decision quickly. In Ford's case, it was the decision to stop producing sedans and double down on trucks and SUVs.

> **Math Trap thinking prevents you from getting bogged down by the details so you can see the range you're in and make a decision quickly.**

We've used reverse Math Trap at Sawyer too. It's why you will not find a Sawyer purifier in retail stores. "Purifier" simply

---

17 Paul A. Eisenstein, "Ford to stop making all passenger cars except the Mustang," updated April 26, 2018, https://www.nbcnews.com/business/autos/ford-stop-making-all-passenger-cars-except-mustang-n869256.

means that it can remove or kill viruses, but viruses are rarely found in water sources used by people around the world.

When it comes to clean water, Sawyer is already one of the big dogs. We know that. We understand our numerator and denominator. This understanding has led us to stay away from certain markets, like water purifiers. It's too small of a market and not worth the investment. We'd spend too much money to pick up too small of a market. The ROI is not worth it. The denominator would be huge relative to the numerator.

Also, the market doesn't need the product. In our view, water purifiers are all marketing hype. (And keep in mind, this is coming from a lifetime marketing guy.) There are no viruses, or very little chance of viruses, in the water that the average people in developing countries or America are going to drink. So, what do you need a purifier for? It is a perception marketers make to sell products to consumers who are not aware of the incredibly low need. Even so, it's a niche that some have carved for themselves. But for Sawyer, the denominator would be too big relative to the numerator. And they really aren't needed for clean drinking water, so we're going to stay out of it.

Before the Tipping Point

Since our first insect repellent hit shelves in 1991, we have converted tens of thousands of people from DEET to picaridin. We're continuing to pick up market share relatively quickly. Big corporations don't want to come into the Sawyer niche because the product is more expensive than DEET, and the DEET market is huge while the picaridin market is still small. The math doesn't work for them yet. But someday the economies of scale will bring costs down as the segment grows. Sawyer doesn't mind the current higher cost because sales are incremental dollars on the way up even if the margins are low. You spend dollars, not margins. Someday it will matter, but not when you're growing. (We'll discuss that in another chapter.) Besides, Sawyer's corporate strategy is to always sell the best available products regardless of the profit margins. We don't need to be number one in the market, but we must be the best on the market.

If we eventually convert enough people away from DEET, there will be a tipping point, probably sometime before hitting 20 percent market share. The big corporations would have to react. They couldn't let a competitor have 20 percent of the pie. If that happens, you can bet it would be war!

How to Make Good Decisions Quickly

I used to simulate baseball games using a deck of cards. I would turn one over and a certain value would represent a fly out. Another value meant that the batter got a single and then another one was a home run. I would just play. I had a league of four teams and I would just sit there and play them and calculate all the stats as I went. Eventually, the numbers became second nature to me. I learned when the numerator was going to move or when the denominator was going to move and what the impact was going to be on the batting average. This childhood pastime eventually led to Math Trap.

Math Trap is a way of thinking that helps you make business decisions quickly. Any well-seasoned executive will know this stuff by nature. It's core strategic thinking. Some people call it "gut feel" because they are basing their decision on years of experience. Math Trap can get you there without having to wait for those years of experience, which are sometimes unpleasant. But I've met many entrepreneurs over the years who need to learn Math Trap. It's a tool that will help you realize the exact math doesn't matter. You lock into a range and the strategy for that range is the same whether you're within the low end or the high end of that range. You don't need to sit there and do all the calculations about what tenth of a percent of market share you own.

Math Trap has permeated everything at Sawyer. Almost all of our charts have an element to it. It gets back to a fundamental understanding of when to move the numerator and when to move the denominator because you understand the range of the decision you're making. This kind of thinking has led me and the Sawyer team to achieve not just growth for Sawyer, and not just good marketing strategy, but it has freed us to make wise philanthropic decisions that change the world.

Fifteen Years of Good Decisions: A Quinceañera for Clean Water

We've had people tell us that our claims about Sawyer water filters seem "too good to be true." Can they really remove 99.99999 percent of harmful bacteria, 99.9999 percent of protozoa, and 100 percent of microplastics? (And is our research *really* that exact?) If so, what kind of impact do the filters really make? Do they last as long as we claim—ten years or more with a lifetime warranty? Do they really change the lives of the people who receive them? Or do they just get thrown out?

I understand these questions. I'm truly amazed by what Sawyer water filters can do too. Fortunately, in addition to our published research that backs up our claims,[18] more than a few folks have endeavored to find some answers.

Sister Larraine Lauter is one such person. Sister Larraine is the cofounder and director of a nonprofit ministry called Water By Women (formerly known as Water With Blessings). In 2006, she traveled with a group of colleagues to various impoverished countries to provide medical care. "Year after year on their medical mission trips, they'd found themselves treating the same illnesses, caused mostly by ingesting unsanitary water. They'd felt helpless. Instead of addressing the problem, they were merely treating symptoms."[19]

They wanted to find a simple, affordable, and reliable solution that they could give to mothers in the various communities they visited, believing that through mothers they would have the greatest chance at making an impact in the whole community. "A chance encounter at a 2007 mission conference led to the Sawyer PointONE water filtration system. The friends knew immediately that their technology problem was solved."[20] Not long after, Sister Larraine began training women in Tegucigalpa, Honduras, on how to use the Sawyer International Bucket System. Water By Women has worked steadily in Honduras since.

They also expanded to do similar work in forty-seven other countries around the world, training and providing filters to more than one hundred thousand "water women," the name given to those who receive a filter. Each water woman is expected to use

---

18 www.sawyer.com/certification
19 "Our Story," Water By Women, accessed February 7, 2024, https://waterbywomen.org/our-story/.
20 "Our Story," Water By Women, accessed February 7, 2024, https://waterbywomen.org/our-story/.

their filter for three other families too. They estimate that the average household size includes three people. This means we can estimate that anywhere from three hundred thousand to 1.2 million people have been given access to safe, clean drinking water through Water By Women. If anyone can verify that the Sawyer water filters are indeed *not* "too good to be true," Sister Larraine is surely among them.

Another woman who endeavored to answer the question, "What kind of impact do these filters really make?" is the YouTube filmmaker and social media influencer Miranda Webster. On her channel, *Miranda Goes Outside!!*, she makes videos about all the things an "outdoorsy" person would love, from hiking and camping gear review videos to travelogues and tips for better experiences in the great outdoors.

Since 2023 was the fifteenth anniversary of Water By Women's work in Honduras, they decided to throw a quinceañera for the organization and the "Mujer del Agua," water women, they work with. A traditional quinceañera is a special celebration thrown on a girl's fifteenth birthday in many Latin American cultures. It's a celebration of the transition from childhood to adulthood. Sister Larraine arranged the celebration, and hundreds of mothers and grandmothers and their families showed up, including ten of the very first women in Honduras who received Sawyer water filters. We invited Miranda and her film crew to travel to Honduras with us to document the celebration.[21]

Together, Sister Larraine and Miranda were able to find fully functioning Sawyer water filters that were fifteen years old and

---

21 Miranda Webster, "Why This is the Last Water Filter I'll Ever Buy!," Miranda Goes Outside!!, May 7, 2023, https://www.youtube.com/watch?v=IY04s2RjFQo.

still safely filtering water. These filters had been backflushed properly and otherwise well cared for. On the same trip, they met with another water woman who was able to start a small business making and selling tortillas because of her filter. Miranda summed up her experience participating in multiple trainings, seeing live GIS surveys on old filters, and seeing the joy on people's faces at the quinceañera with poignant, tearful statements: "These women are just, like, *incredible*. It's just an amazing thing to see these women who now have this super important responsibility to their families and to the homes around them. They are taking it super seriously. It's so clearly this, like . . . *calling*." Miranda went on to say, "Understanding that this thing that I bought at a store, and like scanned and purchased and threw in my pack and never cleaned is here in *this* community. The Sawyer Squeeze water filter is not just some fun toy that I have in my backpack so my water tastes good. This is about saving lives."

Chapter Five

Making Decisions

What are the best business decisions you've ever made? What are the decisions you look back on with confidence, knowing that the call you made led your company, your team, or your product to success?

Verne Harnish, founder of the Young Entrepreneurs' Organization, wrote a book called *The Greatest Business Decisions of All Time*.[22] In it, he lists what he considers to be the top eighteen decisions business leaders have ever made. These decisions include Jack Welch creating a training center (which eventually led to "the GE Way"), Apple rehiring Steve Jobs, and Henry Ford doubling employee salaries to ensure that they could afford the products they were making.[23] Without ques-

---

22 Verne Harnish, *The Greatest Business Decisions of All Time* (Chicago: TI Inc. Books, 2012).
23 As reported by *Forbes*. Kevin Kruse, "The Top 5 Business Decisions Of All Time," May 22, 2013, https://www.forbes.com/sites/kevinkruse/2013/05/22/business-decisions/?sh=7765dd782503.

tion, GE, Apple, and Ford went on to experience incredible business growth after these decisions. But making decisions isn't easy. So how do we do it? How can we ensure that we're making the best call for our businesses? That's what this chapter is all about. We're going to discuss some general principles for making good decisions.

Never Do Something without Reasons Not To

There is a story that gets told in MBA programs that's worth sharing again here. I heard it on my first day at Northwestern.

In the 1960s a man named Alfred P. Sloan was the president of General Motors. He was one of a handful of leaders who changed the automotive industry in the '30s, '40s, '50s, and '60s, ultimately laying the foundation for what it would become today. The story goes that Mr. Sloan was holding a board meeting. Near the end of the meeting, someone suggested a new idea and everyone was in complete agreement about it. The board was ready to move forward unanimously. What could be better? Sloan is said to have responded with: "If we are all in agreement on the decision – then I propose we postpone further discussion of this matter until our next meeting, to give ourselves time to *develop disagreement* and perhaps *gain understanding of what the decision is all about*" (emphasis added).[24]

Why? Because there are no perfect business decisions. There are *always* reasons that you shouldn't do something. There are always

---

[24] Frank Fabela, "What Every Leader Can Learn From Alfred P. Sloan About Tough Decisions," *Fortune*, December 7, 2015, https://fortune.com/2015/12/07/alfred-p-sloan-decision-making/. Various versions of Mr. Sloan's quote can be found online and in other books. The point stands regardless of his exact phrasing.

headwinds you'll have to face. It's better to know what they will be before you set things in motion.

> It's better to know what your headwinds are before you set things in motion.

This doesn't mean that you don't make the decision at all. It just means that you wait until you know why you *shouldn't* before you actually do it. You figure out what your challenges will be ahead of time and start preparing to manage them.

When we first released the Sawyer International Bucket System, our filter included a virus filter. It was harder to use and cost three times more than the Sawyer Squeeze Water Filtration System that we use on our bucket systems today. But we thought we needed to filter out viruses, so we included it.

Dr. Ray Norman, who holds a PhD in Agricultural and Biological Engineering from Cornell University, took our new bucket system to Malawi and came back with the advice to skip the virus filter and use the Squeeze because viruses are rarely in drinking water. Viruses are instead airborne and in bodily fluids. Their survival rate in water is low unless it's in the water that most people don't drink, e.g., warm water that contains raw sewage from a person with hepatitis. This conversation with Dr. Norman was a turning point in the history of Sawyer water filters. Removing the virus filter would make all of our filters less expensive and easier to use. The ripple effect of this decision was bigger than we could've realized in that moment. However, we'd face a "headwind" if we made this change. Public perception was (and still is) that viruses are a major problem in drinking water. Marketers from other companies exploit this perception to sell their filters.

It took millions of dollars in research, as well as considerable time, to prove that a virus filter wasn't needed. But we knew this going into the change and still decided to use the Squeeze on our bucket system rather than the more expensive virus filter. We knew the science backed us up and that our consumers of early educators and early innovators would value that and eventually understand the change. They did and the Sawyer International Bucket System has since been used by millions of people for producing clean, drinkable water.

Perhaps the General Motors board member that day proposed a new car design or a radical new place to put cupholders in an automobile. (Probably not, but who knows.) Regardless, the story goes that, after Mr. Sloan did not approve the proposal because no one could give him a reason not to, it never came up again at any future board meeting.

There are no perfect business decisions. Even if you're 90 percent sure you should make a certain decision, it benefits you and your organization to understand the 10 percent that says "here are reasons not to do it" before you do it.

Seek Opposite Opinions

In Chapter Three we discussed how important it is for entrepreneurs to get rejected at least three times before they get their financing. Helpful dissension may identify possible unintended consequences while you still have time to make adjustments. Doing so also helps entrepreneurs find their niche in the market they're seeking to get into. Similarly, even if you're not in startup mode, you need to seek opposite opinions for every significant decision you make. You need to find people who think about things differently. How do you find these people? The best way is to build a team of them.

While I was at Northwestern, I took a class on strategic thinking. Our professor showed a movie in which the boss was kind of a bully. Everybody on the team said yes to whatever he demanded. Then the professor asked the class, "Should you hire people that think like you? Wouldn't that be the best way to conduct your business?" Numerous students said yes to his leading question.

"No," I said. "That's the last thing in the world you want to do." Why? Because when everyone agrees with you, you will go over the cliff together, unaware that it was even there in the first place. Ideally, you want to hire people who think for themselves and who will give you honest dissension. They still need to believe in the big picture. They still need to be with you. My professor said it best: "You should never ever hire clones."

While you need to hire people who will give you an opposite opinion, you still need to create a team that is headed in the same direction. Everyone still has to believe in the common goal; some people may just think there might be a different path to get there. This is an important balance because, in the end, when the decision is made, everyone on the team needs to get behind it. The team can't afford to have someone grousing that their path wasn't taken. It's helpful to remind people that even when your decision is different than the one they would've made, their contribution was still valuable. Their opposite opinion probably altered your final decision somehow. They probably identified a headwind for you and ultimately helped the team be better prepared for the future.

Think through Causal Effects

Years ago, I was scheduled for my annual review at General Electric. I thought I had a strong grasp on how to think through causal effects, unintended consequences, and other things like that. So, I wrote that in my review—"I'm pretty good at understanding causal effects"— and gave it to my boss's secretary.

Well, the secretary thought I'd written it wrong and she changed *causal* to *casual*. The day of my review came and I went in to see the bosses.

"So, Kurt," they said, "we see that it says here that you're pretty good at understanding *casual effects,* huh? You must be a real party animal!"

I am about the farthest thing from a party animal you can get! My bosses knew that and we had a good laugh.

You might be thinking that this is a good example of causal effect. The secretary changed the word on my employee review (the cause), which changed the start of the conversation in my review (the effect). But causal effect is more than just understanding that A affects B. Causal effect is about asking *how much of* B will change A?

Let's say you're trying to decide if you should raise your price or lower your price. A causal effect might be that if you take your price down, you won't be able to get it back up when you need to. You need to consider questions like:

- What will the price change do to the marketplace?
- If I decide to sell something for $19.99 instead of $29.99, how much will I be leaving on the table?
- Will I get the volume to make up the difference?

- What's it going to do to the competition? Will you drag them all down with you in a race to the bottom, and then collectively no one can get back up because you established that new, lower price point? (Exercise caution here.)
- Will the consumer think that the lower price equals lower quality?

An example of causal effects can be seen in the candy bar business. If you were a candy bar company, what would you do with inflation? You want your candy bars at a certain price point so people will keep buying them on impulse in the grocery store aisle. Some companies are now making them smaller in order to avoid significant price changes.

But there's a limit to how much smaller you can go before you lose your consumers. Plus, if you make them smaller, consider what that will do to your factory. You'll need to recalibrate all the machines to change the size, you'll need all new packaging, all new boxes, etc. You'll have to do all of that to keep the price point while saving on the product.

Other companies are answering inflation by selling two or three packs. "Get three chocolate bars in every pack!" If this approach is taken enough, it destroys the consumer's understanding of the original price. The consumer can no longer remember the price of a single chocolate bar, nor can they figure it out now. Meanwhile, the candy company is hoping to get extra money for putting two or three bars together.

These are critical decisions with causal effects. What will your decision do to your factory? What will it do to the marketplace? Thinking all that stuff through is very important. In the case of candy bars, we have companies making one of two decisions. One is more of a marketing decision: they try to cover up the cost. The other is more of a cost decision: they try to lower their costs because inflation is hitting. (The same thing is happening with cereal boxes, ice cream cartons, and individual yogurt containers. Take a look next time you go grocery shopping. Do you know how big each of those items is anymore? Do you know how much they should cost? Is there less product in the same size box or container?)

At this point you may also be wondering, aren't causal effects the same thing as Creative Destruction? No, they're not. Understanding Creative Destruction in your business is about looking for big, new opportunities. Causal effects are more mundane, though they can be just as important.

Every decision will have a long-term effect that you may or may not be able to get back from, so you have to think these things through. It's like the old game of dominoes. Once you set things in motion, you may not be able to control the effects or reverse course. So, think through the causal effects of your decisions before you make them.

In Chapter Four, I shared the story about how we intentionally put the word *picaridin* on the packaging of our picaridin repellent while our competitors spent time investing in their brand names. As picaridin became more popular with the CDC, they started to show our product more than others because of the way it was named. It was great publicity for us. And over time, other companies have started to put picaridin on their packaging too. This was a causal effect, both the good publicity and the change in packaging within the marketplace. We're still thinking through what this means for us and our picaridin repellents. You can't ignore causal effects.

Deciding *Not* to Automate Production: Responding to Disaster

Something that sets Sawyer apart from other manufacturers is that we have built our factory for flexibility. To do so, we pay a little more in labor and we have to carry extra inventory. In order to change the production lines from one product to another quickly, we give up some automation options that would make our normal production a little faster and a little cheaper.

For example, on our repellent filling lines, we still have people handloading bottles on and off the conveyor belt. For speed, many companies would have switched a long time ago to automatic loaders and unloaders. But what they gain in efficiency they lose in flexibility. Why is flexibility important to us? Because we want to be able to help people *quickly* when disaster strikes.

Sawyer can respond to any disaster in the world because of our flexibility in production. When there is a natural disaster, we are one of the first calls for NGOs, relief organizations, and even the US government. We simply *must* be flexible enough to crank out orders for one hundred thousand or more filters to be shipped *tomorrow*. I'm not exaggerating. I opened this book with stories about relief efforts in Haiti and Puerto Rico. Both of those natural disasters required that we were able to manufacture more than one hundred thousand filters each (the orders for Puerto Rico were over 175,000) and be ready to ship them very quickly. Similarly, we once received a call from the military on a Friday.

The person I spoke with said, "We'll take every repellent you have. We're leaving tomorrow at 10 a.m." In another situation, the military called just two days after a terrorist strike halfway around the world. We shipped thousands of filters the *same day* to a war-torn area where civilians needed water.

I'm not sharing these stories so everyone at Sawyer can pat themselves on the back. However, these are good examples of the kind of world-changing things you can do with your organization when you have (1) built solid relationships with like-minded organizations; (2) built your factory for flexibility; and (3) know what your values are.

So, it costs us a few pennies more per unit to operate this way. With people, we can change a line in fifteen minutes versus the *four hours* it would take with an automated line. (Talk about a causal effect!) Fortunately, we have strong enough operating margins to allow for this kind of operation.

This brings me back to knowing your values. At Sawyer, we value generosity and changing the real lives of other people. I've tried to build that into the Sawyer ethos by making wise decisions (as we discussed above) and by hiring others who share the same passion. We're not perfect, but we're truly trying to be "more than an outdoor company." So, why wouldn't we use some of the operating margin to ensure that our factory is flexible? If we had not, then we couldn't help people in their moments of greatest need.

Chapter Six

The Decision Matrix

Have you ever noticed that most people make a decision based on just one or two variables that they feel a strong emotion about?

"I want to eat at McDonald's instead of Burger King because I really like the french fries at McDonald's."

Choosing a fast-food restaurant is a pretty inconsequential decision, but human behavior is to make big decisions the same way.

"I prefer this house over the other because I just love the backyard."

"I want to go to this college instead of the other four I've been considering because it has a program I like and the best-tasting food."

"I want to give money to this charity over the others because their story of helping the little kids made me cry!"

None of this is "wrong" necessarily, but all of these decisions include more variables than the one or two mentioned.

Also, there is no guarantee that any of these decisions are truly the best or wisest decisions to make.

We started a conversation about decision-making in the last chapter, but I'd like to drill down deeper. In this chapter, I want to introduce you to a helpful tool I have used for years on every kind of decision you can think of: the Decision Matrix.

I've used the Decision Matrix at Sawyer. I've used it at home. I've used it with my kids to help them pick which college they would attend. I have even used it (when I was asked) to talk people into getting married and to talk others out of getting married. What makes this such a valuable tool is that it takes the emotions out of your decision. The matrix helps you address every variable—especially the variables you're probably overlooking—and not simply those that you feel strongly about.

Before we begin, one caveat: using the Decision Matrix does not provide a guarantee. Even as we practice future thinking, we can't make guarantees about every decision we make in life or business. For people of faith, we must leave the future up to God. However, the Decision Matrix can certainly help us make wiser, more informed decisions. It often leads people to surprising results, even causing them to choose what they once thought was their third or fourth choice instead of their first. Let's take a look at some examples.

Let's say you were a student about to head to college and you were seriously considering four schools. You would begin by putting the names (or a variable representing each name) above columns 3, 5, 7, and 9. Above columns 4, 6, 8, and 10 you can simply write "Score." For this example, we'll use an abbreviated matrix that our oldest son, Brian, used to select his college.

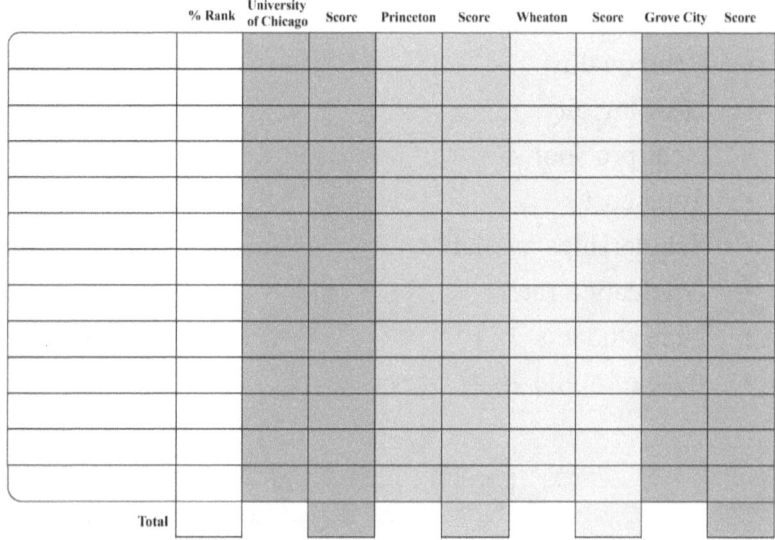

In the first column, you're going to list thirteen variables for making your decision. Simply label this column "Variables." Lots of people I've spoken with believe that they can't think of that many different variables for every decision. But I've found that if you start writing them down it's easy to come up with thirteen variables and sometimes a lot more. I say a minimum of ten. When I helped my children decide on their colleges, we came up with more than twenty variables. As I said in Chapter Four, we need to spend more time thinking.

Here are the thirteen variables Brian used for choosing his college:

- Academic reputation
- School size (small)
- Undergrad vs. grad ratio
- Majors offered

- Dorm options
- Food quality
- Near big city
- Near pro sports
- Total cost
- Scholarships available
- Graduation rate
- Nice students
- Ease of home visits

	% Rank	University of Chicago	Score	Princeton	Score	Wheaton	Score	Grove City	Score
Academic reputation									
Small school									
Undergrad vs grad									
Majors offered									
Dorm options									
Food quality									
Near big city									
Near pro sports									
Cost									
Scholarships									
Graduation rate									
Nice students									
Ease of home visits									
Total									

Now that the four choices are listed and we've identified thirteen variables for making the decision, we can really begin to use this matrix.

The next task is to decide how important each one of those variables is to you. You're asking yourself, "How big of a piece of the decision does this need to be?" You do this by assigning numeric values to each decision in column 2. The total of the values must equal one hundred.

Brian determined that getting a computer and technology-based degree is a high priority and so assigned eight points to the row "Majors offered." The cost of tuition was a serious consideration too, and so he assigned another fifteen points to that row. Brian wasn't overly concerned with what city the school is located in, so he assigned five points to that row. Brian is also easy to please when it comes to food and assigned a five to "Food quality." The longer he went about this process, the easier it was for him to come up with the other values. After a few minutes of thinking and making adjustments, he filled in all thirteen rows of column 2.

	% Rank	University of Chicago	Score	Princeton	Score	Wheaton	Score	Grove City	Score
Academic reputation	15								
Small school	10								
Undergrad vs grad	7								
Majors offered	8								
Dorm options	5								
Food quality	5								
Near big city	5								
Near pro sports	3								
Cost	15								
Scholarships	8								
Graduation rate	9								
Nice students	5								
Ease of home visits	5								
Total	100								

Some variables might be so important they get thirty points or even fifty points. That's OK. The idea is not only to see all the variables in play but also to see how they rank against one another based on their point totals. You might find as you begin assigning points that some variables are more important to you than you first realized.

The next step is to assess the quality of each variable within each of the four options. We do this by assigning a value of one to ten. Back to Brian's matrix, the cost for Princeton is at the very top end of his comfort zone, so that particular school got three out of ten in the "Cost" row. Meanwhile, the tuition for Grove City was much more doable, so he awarded it an eight out of ten in the "Cost" row. Brian continued to rate every variable at every potential school on a scale of one to ten.

	% Rank	University of Chicago	Score	Princeton	Score	Wheaton	Score	Grove City	Score
Academic reputation	15	10		10		8		8	
Small school	10	8		6		10		8	
Undergrad vs grad	7	5		6		7		9	
Majors offered	8	10		8		8		8	
Dorm options	5	8		4		9		8	
Food quality	5	8		7		8		8	
Near big city	5	10		7		10		2	
Near pro sports	3	10		7		10		3	
Cost	15	6		3		5		8	
Scholarships	8	8		7		5		0	
Graduation rate	9	8		7		9		9	
Nice students	5	10		4		9		10	
Ease of home visits	5	7		2		7		3	
Total	100								

The next step is to multiply the value of each variable at each school by the total points that variable is worth. The product is put in the score column for each school: C2 × C3 = C4; C2 × C5 = C6; etc.

	% Rank	University of Chicago	Score	Princeton	Score	Wheaton	Score	Grove City	Score
Academic reputation	15	10	150	10	150	8	120	8	120
Small school	10	8	80	6	60	10	100	8	80
Undergrad vs grad	7	5	35	6	42	7	49	9	63
Majors offered	8	10	80	8	64	8	64	8	64
Dorm options	5	8	40	4	20	9	45	8	40
Food quality	5	8	40	7	35	8	40	8	40
Near big city	5	10	50	7	35	10	50	2	10
Near pro sports	3	10	30	7	21	10	30	3	9
Cost	15	6	90	3	45	5	75	8	120
Scholarships	8	8	64	7	56	5	40	0	0
Graduation rate	9	8	72	7	63	9	81	9	81
Nice students	5	10	50	4	20	9	45	10	50
Ease of home visits	5	7	35	2	10	7	35	3	15
Total	100								

Now that every cell in the matrix is filled in, the final step is to total the scores.

	% Rank	University of Chicago	Score	Princeton	Score	Wheaton	Score	Grove City	Score
Academic reputation	15	10	150	10	150	8	120	8	120
Small school	10	8	80	6	60	10	100	8	80
Undergrad vs grad	7	5	35	6	42	7	49	9	63
Majors offered	8	10	80	8	64	8	64	8	64
Dorm options	5	8	40	4	20	9	45	8	40
Food quality	5	8	40	7	35	8	40	8	40
Near big city	5	10	50	7	35	10	50	2	10
Near pro sports	3	10	30	7	21	10	30	3	9
Cost	15	6	90	3	45	5	75	8	120
Scholarships	8	8	64	7	56	5	40	0	0
Graduation rate	9	8	72	7	63	9	81	9	81
Nice students	5	10	50	4	20	9	45	10	50
Ease of home visits	5	7	35	2	10	7	35	3	15
Total	100		816		621		774		692

It turns out that in this example the University of Chicago scored 816 points while Princeton scored 621 points. Wheaton scored 774 and Grove City scored 692. Now this is when the matrix becomes really valuable. If Brian had looked only at the top two things, he would have decided between the University of Chicago and Grove City. But when he looked at the whole picture, he realized that he should be picking between the University of Chicago and Wheaton. The little things add up.

In this way, the Decision Matrix reveals *hidden preferences.* It helps you discover an opportunity you wouldn't have thought of before.

Once you realize what your final two choices are, you go back and do it again fresh. You reassess your scores as well as your one-to-ten values for your top two choices. Why? Because there's often a significant difference in the scores. Working through this process differentiates what is very important from what is just of mild importance.

A score like 860 is going to become 920 or 740. It will move. These shifting scores will help you sort out the best from the second best. When you use the Decision Matrix, you will typically get a bunch of 600s, maybe a 700, and then at least two or three options that will score higher than the rest.

We used the Decision Matrix to help our first three kids determine which college to go to. (The decision for the fourth was a no-brainer.) Each of my kids had different variables and different values for the variables. For example, with our daughter Gwen, who played college basketball, there were team and coach quality questions. For Brian, it came down to the University of Chicago and Wheaton very quickly. The

University of Chicago won out, though Wheaton was a close runner-up.

Rocking Chair Theory

Our example so far has been that of a teenager deciding on which college she wants to go to. But what if you're in midlife or older and you're facing a big decision? For those of us in the second half of life, we may want to consider something I've shared with many others around Sawyer: the Rocking Chair Theory.

The idea is simple: Imagine that you're an older person sitting on your rocking chair, enjoying the sunset with a cat in your lap or a cup of tea or whatever makes you comfortable, and you're reflecting on your life. What are the things that you wish you had done? Tour the country in an RV with your spouse? Visit Europe? Move out of the city and buy a home in the country? To avoid regret, I think it's wise for one or more variables in a Decision Matrix to somehow reflect a lifelong goal and then to give that variable a significant weight, maybe even 20 percent.

For example, a friend of mine who is past midlife bought two acres of land where he intended to build a house to retire in. (What he called his "final" home.) He went through all the normal permitting processes. Everything was set to break ground.

A week before the crews were scheduled to start building, his next-door neighbor told my friend that she was putting her house up for sale. Were he to purchase her home, it would give him an additional 6.5 acres, plus a really nice house that was already built. My friend immediately agreed to his neighbor's price and contacted the bank. Unfortunately, the appraisal came back for considerably less than the neighbor's asking price. The bank would not finance what he wanted and he started getting cold feet on the deal.

He couldn't reach a decision. My friend identified all the variables he could think of and then ran the Decision Matrix. The matrix pointed to sticking with his original plan—settle on two acres and build a new home, but the Rocking Chair Theory said they should move into his neighbor's old house, even if it would cost him more upfront.

I said to him, "Think about down the road, when you have the house built and you are sitting on your front porch in your rocking chair looking at the house next door. Are you going to be constantly regretting it?"

After giving it some thought, my friend said, "You're right!" He decided that it was worth taking more out of his savings and buying the property. I heard him say once, "That was the best advice and decision of my life."

Rocking Chair Theory may sound like introducing an emotional element back into the Decision Matrix, but it's not. It's not making a bad choice over a good choice, but rather choosing between two good choices. Rocking Chair Theory factors in how you would like to reflect upon your life choices when you're old. It helps you avoid regrets by significantly weighting the variables that point to your lifelong goals.

You don't have to be old to benefit from Rocking Chair Theory. Some big decisions come early in life: Public school versus private or homeschooling? Save money on college or invest in a more expensive college that better reflects your core values? You can use the Rocking Chair Theory when you're young.

A Tale of Two Couples

I mentioned that I've used the Decision Matrix to both talk people into and out of marriage. This might seem strange, but for the people I spoke with, it was an eye-opener! Think of all the variables to marriage, some of which people tend not to think about right away.

- Who will your in-laws be and what will they expect?
- What are the financial realities of each person?
- Is anyone bringing significant debt or other financial problems into the marriage?
- Do you know where you want to live and work?
- How many kids does each person expect to have?

The list goes on.

One couple I counseled was an American man and a Vietnamese woman. The young woman was one of the best interns we've ever had at Sawyer. She asked me to walk her and her fiancé through the Decision Matrix. They filled them out separately then discussed their scores. They scored perfectly on almost every variable except where to live. She wanted to return to Vietnam at least once for a period of time during her career but he did not. The Decision Matrix brought this discussion to the surface and helped them see that this decision was a very important thing they had to settle before they got married.

For this couple, the Decision Matrix revealed a potential deal-breaker. We don't always realize we have a deal-breaker until all the variables are accounted for. Deal-breakers don't exist in every decision, but when they do, you'll be glad to sort them out *before* a final decision is made.

I'm happy to report that this couple ended up working it out. They got married, they're still happy and together, and they have plans to visit Vietnam.

But I had another guy visit my office with questions about his potential marriage too. He was a key employee at Sawyer for many years and someone for whom I was a mentor. After walking through the Decision Matrix, he decided *not* to get married. He has thanked me for that conversation ever since.

What Successful Business Owners Need to Ask Themselves

This leads me to an important question that every successful entrepreneur or business owner should be asking themselves: *Do I need, or do I want, to go big and take my company public?*

If you do, you can't do what I'm doing. You can't be as radically generous as Sawyer has been because you've given up control of the company. If you're thinking of selling someday, use the Decision Matrix. It's an incredible tool and totally free. (See Appendix A for a template.) Make sure to include variables for generosity and philanthropy.

What Entrepreneurs Need to Ask Themselves

You may not be anywhere near selling your company. You might be deciding if you want to open a new restaurant or start a venture. Use this tool. For the would-be restaurant owner, ask yourself:

- Do I have a good location?
- Can I produce good food?
- Is there demand for my food?

- How will I get people into my restaurant?
- How will I promote?
- Do I specialize or have a big menu?
- How will I track where people are coming from?
- How will I be able to pay my employees?

You could do this matrix across the menu itself, assessing each entree you plan to offer. Or you could use the matrix to determine your location. It's a versatile tool.

Perhaps you're a manufacturer and you need to choose among a handful of distributors. Perhaps you need to purchase new vehicles for your business and each option brings a host of variables with it. Or perhaps you need to hire a new independent sales rep and you have four options.

You could take it further. Each one of the Four Ps of Marketing could be run through the Decision Matrix. Think of all the questions that come with product, price, presence, and promotion. *Do you have a great product? Should you give out samples? Should you hire someone to run social media? Do you know if it's best to price high or low?* And on and on.

The Decision Matrix helps you look at the whole picture and think of things you would not have thought about. By the time you have run your options through the matrix a couple of times you add subjectivity to your emotions.

Get It in Your Head

I've run variables through the Decision Matrix so much that it's just in my head. I no longer have to put my words on paper, but I think this way all the time. I am always trying to think through all the variables. I use it for personal decisions as well as business and philanthropy decisions. It's fundamental to every marketing decision and fundamental to much of life too.

For new business or charitable initiatives, I think through questions like: *Do we have people with the right skill sets? Do we have the financial resources in place?* Or if the decision is more personal in nature. I might think, *Is my wife, Barb, in support of this? Is my family in support of this? Will God support me with this thing?*

The Decision Matrix will help you identify the little pitfalls of various decisions you will make at your company. Take the time to rank all the variables you can think of. Never let the top two things make your decision. Go through the whole process and allow your emotions about a decision to rest while the variables are scored. You might be surprised by which option rises to the top.

This doesn't mean I make flawless decisions. I have made a lot of mistakes in my time. Let me tell you a story about a recent one.

A Skirmish over Shelf Space

There was another instance when I let my emotions get in the way of good decision-making. One of our competitors came out with a new water filter that allowed you to pump directly from the stream. It got hot quickly. It won new product awards in some of the camping and hiking media and it was widely discussed online. It seemed to be getting endorsements and accolades from everyone.

In response to this fanfare, some retailers took our filters off the shelf to make room for the competition. I have a competitive gene in me that goes back to playing sports. When someone starts taking our shelf space, I get serious.

So, we rushed out our version of the product. We spent a fair bit of money on it, but we probably shouldn't have spent a penny. One year later, neither product was on the shelves anymore, not the competition's and not our rushed version. We'd regained our shelf space with the high-performance Sawyer water filters we're known for.

The competition's product wasn't a good product. I should've known that eventually it would die because it didn't meet the needs of the public. The filter we made in response wasn't great either. Had I used the Decision Matrix, I would've seen that my emotions were driving me—that diehard competitive nature—and I would've made a different decision, saving both time and money. Unfortunately, this wasn't the only time I let my emotions drive my decision-making.

Shark Tank

We released the Sawyer Extractor ™ Pump Kit in 1984. Right away there were copycat products on the market trying to compete with us. They attempted to gain market share from us but it didn't last. We had the product that no one could match (part of what we call "The Sawyer Standard") and it won out. The competition just faded away. We didn't hear from them again for years.

Then, in a 2019 episode of *Shark Tank,* two entrepreneurs proposed an extractor-like product—the same one we vanquished in the late 1980s. It's a cheap tool that will suck bug venom only. They managed to get host Lori Greiner to back them.[25] It was the same old product all over again, a cheaper and less effective device for retrieving venom.

---

25 "Lori Offers A Golden Ticket To Bug Bite Thing | Shark Tank Global," Shark Tank Global, September 29, 2022, https://www.youtube.com/watch?v=lfzoGrzFn2g.

While I knew this competition wasn't going to last long, I didn't want to underestimate the power of *Shark Tank*. Plus, they were going to be directly targeting Sawyer's customers. If they were successful, they might even take a large retail partner like Walmart from us. So, I went into protective mode. I immediately tooled our manufacturing to produce a less expensive Extractor™ Pump Kit and called it the Extractor™ Mini.

In hindsight, I rushed this decision. Retooling our manufacturing is not a small operation. It can sometimes take six months of lead time.

In the end, this new product never got off the shelf. We knew they were selling a lot of them to retailers, maybe a million, but the people weren't actually buying them in great quantities. All they did was fill pipelines. They never went out the door. A little bit was sold on Amazon, but nothing that seriously threatened the Sawyer Extractor™ Pump Kit or necessitated our rush to create an Extractor™ Mini. They must have had to take a lot of them back. Eventually it left the market.

But Sawyer was ready. We got the Mini all tooled up. We actually made improvements on it in the process. We had a new manual written, describing what every bite is, how to treat it, and how to avoid further problems.

We even offered it to Walmart where the full Pump Kit was already on shelves. We told them they could take the full kit out and substitute it with the new, lower-cost Extractor™ Mini. (The minis didn't treat snake bites, just bee stings and mosquito bites.) But in the end, they didn't take any customers, so we never had to pull the full Extractor™ Pump Kit out.

If I had slowed down, I would've had the wisdom to predict their lack of success and make it a significant variable in my Decision Matrix. But I was in protective mode, making some decisions emotionally, rather than thinking through every potential outcome. I didn't want the Walmart buyer to say, "Well, let me take out this sixteen-dollar product and put it in a six-dollar product." If that was going to happen, then I was determined that it would be *our* six-dollar product, not Lori Greiner's. (Acting to protect a core Sawyer product was not entirely "wrong," and we did develop a useful bug manual with it that we can use elsewhere.)

The Decision Matrix takes your emotions out of the decision and introduces variables you aren't focused on. It's a tool that will elevate your decision-making.

Are you a professional decision-maker? Or are you an emotional decision-maker? Can you get past the two things that are stuck in your head and make a good decision?

> **Are you a professional decision-maker?**
> **Or are you an emotional decision-maker?**

They Meant It for Evil, But . . .

We had just gotten into the water filter business in 2003. We sourced our new filters from a local company in Florida that also worked with an outside supplier in Japan. One day the owner of the Florida company called me to say that he could no longer afford to pay his two key employees. I told him to send them to Sawyer. We put them on Sawyer's payroll. In this way, we could continue to develop our new water filters and he could continue to use them as needed. So, over they came. One of these employees was John Smith.

Two weeks later, the owner of the Florida company sued us for stealing his employees and even went as far as to forge supposedly signed noncompete clauses. His announced goal was to take control of Sawyer. We knew that the employees had not signed noncompete clauses, and we eventually prevailed in arbitration after very expensive legal fees for our small company.

When it came time for us to order more filter elements, their Japanese supplier told us that they could not sell to us due to the threat of another lawsuit by the owner of the Florida company. Even though we had just defeated them in court, their supplier was unwilling to do business with us. Fortunately, John had been working with this supplier before he joined Sawyer and had taken the time to develop real relationships with each of his contacts. He knew their names, knew their spouses, and knew all about them. One salesperson from the Japanese supplier gave John the name of another supplier who could meet Sawyer's needs. It turned out that this new supplier produced components for our water filters that were far superior! Though the change was forced upon us, we now had an *even better* water filter than before.

After more than twenty years, no competitor has been able to match our proprietary secret formula for the filter. Meanwhile, John eventually became our vice president of operations, and he continues to play a critical role in Sawyer's success. While the Florida company that threatened our first supplier with a lawsuit meant it for evil, God used it for good. The filters made with parts from the first supplier would not have saved thousands of lives, nor would it have changed millions of more lives as our current filters have done and continue to do.

Chapter Seven

The Circle of Customers

You have probably heard it said that "the easiest way to build your business is by selling more things to the same people." That's a core marketing concept you'll hear in nearly any business seminar or read in most business books. It's the original way of thinking. It's a valuable concept, but I like to put a little spin on it called The Circle of Customers. Your customers (or if you're a nonprofit, your donors) can be grouped into three main categories—loyal, casual, and fringe.

Your loyal customers are those who are already buying your products.

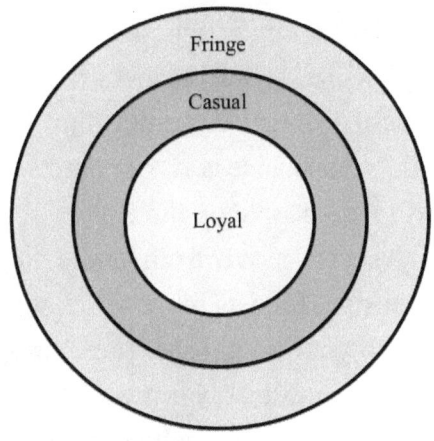

The Circle of Customers

You might think of them as your loyal base. They may have signed up for your newsletter. They may also follow one of your social media accounts. They rave about your product or service or humanitarian efforts to their friends. They've purchased your good or service. They like it. And they'll purchase from you again. You may also put key retail partners within the loyal base. (More on this later.)

Casual customers are those I think of as tire kickers. They're walking around the car dealership taking in all the models. They haven't yet climbed inside. They're kicking the tires and peering in through the windows but not yet sitting behind the wheel. They're appraising your company and your product or services from a comfortable, noncommittal distance.

The people on the fringe don't know who you are yet. They don't know your brand. They don't know what you do. They've passed your product in the aisle without looking twice at the packaging.

The question is, now that you have grouped your customers into three categories, how does this help you build your business?

You start by selling more things to your loyal base. The next way to grow your business is to bring in the tire kickers. You move the casual customer into the loyal base. The last way to build your business is, of course, to go out and introduce yourself to the people on the fringe.

As you move from circle to circle, it always gets more expensive. It costs more to sell a product to a tire kicker than it does to your loyal base. It requires more publicity, more advertising, or more social media. When you start reaching for the fringe, then you're really spending money. Focusing on bringing in the fringe can consume a marketing budget quickly, and it isn't the most effective way to grow your business. Instead, start by increasing the loyal base, then focus on the tire kickers, then move to the fringe.

The diagram below indicates the movement of customers from one circle to the next and the growth of that loyal base. The circle gets bigger as you bring people closer to the center. As your loyal base grows, the center circle—and your business—will get larger.

The Circle of Customers applies not only to businesses and non-profits but to colleges too. Sawyer has worked with a number of schools over the years on research projects and clean water initiatives. I've had the pleasure of meeting and speaking with faculty and

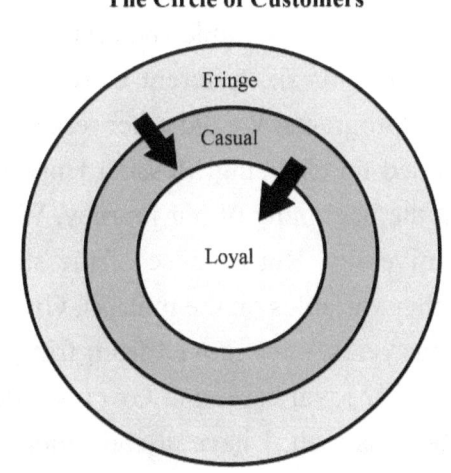

The Circle of Customers

administrators across the country. In recent years, many schools have struggled with making the adjustment to rapidly growing online education. Fewer students are willing to live on campus, so they're not paying for room and board, which decreases the amount of money the school has coming in. It's been a disruption to how higher education has been traditionally done. When I'm in conversation with those in higher ed, I encourage them to think in terms of The Circle of Customers. First, they reach out to the kids of past alumni (the loyal base). Then they focus on the kids who live in the area (the casual tire kickers). As their programs grow, they suddenly have new students discovering them (the fringe).

People on the fringe will discover you as your organization grows and becomes recognized for its work. This was true for my family when it came to picking the right school for my daughter. As I mentioned in Chapter Six, we used the Decision Matrix to help each of our children find the right college for them. For Gwen, playing college basketball at a Christian school was a variable she assigned a high value to. So, we visited five or six different Christian colleges with good basketball programs. We did other research and, after using the matrix, ended up choosing Messiah University. We were on the fringe at the beginning of our journey. We had never heard of Messiah University. But because of the strength of their program (and other variables on the matrix), Gwen played basketball there for four years.[26] We moved from fringe to casual to eventually part of their loyal base, and Gwen's sister, Bethany, went to college there as well. I have already mentioned that Sawyer has since participated in philanthropic projects with Messiah University. This is because we're still in the loyal base all these years later. (We'll discuss some of the exciting work we've done together in Chapter Eleven.)

I said earlier that it's important to include your primary retailers within your loyal base too. For example, Walmart is part of Sawyer's loyal base. At any given time, they carry eight to ten of our products, but years ago they started with just one. Over the years we established a good relationship with them. We

---

[26] They were Division III national runner-ups during her senior year. It was an incredible and memorable season.

got set up in their system, they got our vendor information, and over time we kept adding to the number of Sawyer products that might interest their customers. We assume that the person who uses Sawyer filters might be amenable to buying Sawyer repellents and so on. The same is true for Bass Pro, REI, and others. Through our work with retail partners, we've grown the loyal base for Sawyer Products to probably a couple million people.

The Circle of Customers is how you build the business. You don't just sell more things to the same people. You think of these three layers of customers and move people from one layer to the next.

Lots of entrepreneurs will try to stay with one product or service alone. It's their baby, and like any proud parent, they want everyone to know how amazing she is. So, they spend all their time and money trying to find new customers. I understand this inclination, but if you've ever watched *Shark Tank* then you know that entrepreneurs who take this approach are destined to have a customer acquisition problem.

How will you get new customers? What do you need to learn for engaging a new market? How much will it cost? New customers are expensive. You have to spend a lot more money reaching out to the fringe customers as you try to bring them in than you will ever spend adding products that your loyal base will buy. The further you go out in the circle, the more expensive it is to market.

Adapt and Survive

A close friend of mine from Northwestern, Roger Fortier, came to me with what would eventually become the Sawyer Extractor™

Pump Kit. He came across the product in his home country of France. It was an interesting concept: a quick, sudden vacuum meant to remove snake venom. The pump was sold in France under the name Aspivenin, which translates to "Venom Sucker." It was developed and patented by Andre Emerit at the Pasteur Institute for the treatment of bee stings. Roger, Barbara, and I headed off to Paris to secure the US rights to the pump.

On our second day, we met with the Aspivenin folks and then scheduled a trip to the manufacturing plant in Lyon for day four. In between, Barbara made a crude mockup of a blister-carded unit. In France, the pump was sold by pharmacists in their small Green Cross Pharmacies. It was positioned for bee stings as there is no venomous snake problem in France.

Day four came and we were all on France's high-speed rail service, the TGV train, whipping through the countryside at 200 mph. We showed them the crude blister card. They reached across the table with a handshake and proclaimed, "We will do business."

That settled, we came back to the US with a focus on drugstores because that was how they were sold in France. We got a few nibbles from southern drugstore chains but not enough to sustain a business. However, snake bite kits were sold in all camping departments across the US. We verified with research at the University of Arizona (with the foremost snake bite expert in the world) that our pump worked on snake bites too. So, our product became more associated with snake bites than bee stings. It was a slam dunk as big box stores, sporting goods chains, independent outdoor retailers, and anybody with a camping department signed on.

Camping stores quickly became our focus and we abandoned the propositioning of drugstore chains. We also found some industrial customers, such as those with utility workers who had to traipse across snake-infested fields. We were never able to recapture the bee sting benefits as a main selling point. But, the pump was the start of how Sawyer got to where it is today. Adapt and survive.

When we added the Remote Emergency First Aid Kit in 1985, we started to see the growth of the business we expected to see from our initial travels to drugstores. But it didn't come from new stores carrying Sawyer Products. The business grew because the people who were already purchasing Sawyer Extractor™ Pump Kits had no problem adding our first aid kits to their orders. By 1988, we added Sawyer repellents and sunscreens. Years later, we added water filters.

If you're managing a nonprofit, you can also use The Circle of Customers to think about how you can grow your organization to make a bigger impact. At the center of the circle, your loyal base is comprised of the people you serve. How do you grow that base? How do you use your donor's money more efficiently? How do you make a great impact on the problem you're trying to fight?

Let's say you run a nonprofit that feeds hungry people in impoverished countries. Perhaps you're able to serve meals to 200,000 people every day in Zimbabwe, but you believe you might have the capacity to serve 250,000 meals every day. Is it easier to provide the additional 50,000 meals in Zimbabwe, or should you go to a neighboring country like Mozambique to provide the additional 50,000 meals? How are your relationships there? Instead, you can save money and grow the reach of your nonprofit—i.e., helping real people eat meals—by growing your base in the same country rather than trying to find more people to feed in other countries.

The Circle of Customers approach is how the Sawyer business grew, not by searching for new customers the way many entrepreneurs attempt to, but by selling more things to the same retailers and the same customers who were familiar with the name Sawyer. Thinking about moving customers from one circle to the next and the most effective ways to do that (e.g., earned media over advertising) is what helped me realize how business growth works. It also saved Sawyer the money we would've spent chasing customers on the fringe, allowing us to spend even more on philanthropic projects.

A Social Disruption

Social media was a disruptor to nearly every industry and, in some respects, our whole way of life. It certainly has changed many of the traditional ways we used to market products. In terms of The Circle of Customers, social media has made it easier to bring the tire kickers out of the casual circle and into the loyal base.

A great example of this is the popular outdoor YouTuber Dan Becker, who, like many other outdoor enthusiasts, posted a review video about a Sawyer water filter. In November 2020, Dan Posted a video called "Why the Katadyn BeFree DESTROYS the Sawyer Squeeze Water Filter."[27] In it, Dan compared the water

---

27   Dan Becker, "Why the Katadyn BeFree DESTROYS the Sawyer Squeeze Water Filter," November 12, 2020, https://www.youtube.com/watch?v=JjogXYWufgY.

bags, flow rates, and costs of the Katadyn BeFree Water Filter and the Sawyer Squeeze Water Filtration System. According to Dan, the Katadyn filter was cheaper, included a bag that was easier to use, and had a much faster flow rate than the Sawyer Squeeze. He ended by saying, "This [Katadyn] is *the best water filter I've ever seen.*"

Dan is an entertaining YouTuber with a loyal fanbase.[28] He's also spent a lot of time out on the trail experimenting with different products. His opinions are informed and his videos are fun to watch. So, it was easy for most people to watch that video and think, "I'll never buy a Sawyer filter over a Katadyn."

The problem was that Dan was missing *a lot* of important information about Sawyer—not just the water filter he was reviewing, but about our company's purpose. He was in the casual circle, closer to the fringe than to the loyal base, so we called him up.

Dan was *amazed* to hear about the millions of lives being changed by Sawyer water filters around the world. Learning more about how Sawyer water filters are .01 micron absolute was one thing, but what captured Dan's imagination to learn more about us were the clean water projects we're committed to around the world.

He eventually traveled to Nairobi, Kenya, with Darrel Larson, our International Director, to visit Kibera, one of the largest slums in the world. Darrel's role was to train Kenyans on how to install, clean, and distribute water filters throughout Kibera. Sawyer was participating with The Bucket Ministry to

---

28 Even social media influencers can think of their followers in terms of The Circle of Customers.

try and bring clean water to all 408,000 people in Kibera, which, by the way, is only four square miles. In January 2023, Dan posted a new video called, "EXPOSED – Sawyer Products isn't who you think they are."[29] In this video, Dan took his hundreds of thousands of viewers directly into Kibera. Suddenly, people all over the world saw living conditions they could've never imagined—408,000 people living within four square miles; only seventy-eight toilets in the entire slum; children playing near piles of trash containing human waste and other garbage; contaminated water running down the streets and out of taps. They also witnessed The Bucket Ministry in action and how Sawyer International Bucket System water filters provided clean water to people who had literally never had a clean glass of water to drink before.

Dan ended his video by saying, "Sawyer doesn't care about selling you a water filter. Their end goal is literally to see people's lives change." He captured images of Darrel and local leaders training others on how to effectively clean and use the water filters. He also captured images of people in Kibera worshipping God as they heard the message of salvation in Jesus, which The Bucket Ministry shares wherever they work.

The response to this video was incredible:

- "I don't share the faith, and am often turned off by folks who focus too much on the faith and too little on the acts. This video was AMAZING to watch. Your faith enabled you to relate to the people involved in a way that I could

---

[29] Dan Becker, "EXPOSED - Sawyer Products isn't who you think they are," January 6, 2023, https://www.youtube.com/watch?v=vvqdnFgr5Fg&t=58s.

never do, but all while doing and advocating something palpable. To me, it's like a superpower."
- "Bought a Sawyer a few years ago. I had no idea they do this work. Thank you for showcasing and thank you sawyer for literally making the world a better place ♥♥♥."
- "Though I'm not a religious person, thank you for reminding me that we should help others when we can, so I clicked the link and donated."
- "I'm from Nairobi and I'm glad to see this sort of awareness being created in the international outdoor community."
- "After watching [the video], I felt compelled to donate to Sawyer's foundation. I was just going to do a one-time [donation] of $100, but saw the $20 a month option and used that. I have NEVER done this kind of contribution before."
- "Dude, it brought me to tears . . . May God Bless you for posting this video informing all of us how lucky we are and letting us know who Sawyer is and what they do. I bought the right [water filter] and will continue to support Sawyer."
- "I work for a water utility here in America. Most people don't know the amount of work that goes in to providing clean, healthy water. We are lucky to have a rich country that can provide for its citizens. It is great that we can provide for those less fortunate through a company like Sawyer."
- "Thank you, Dan, I had no idea that Sawyer supported such a role in this community in need. I have bought Sawyer products since I first started hiking/backpacking. I will continue to support Sawyer as long as I live."

- "Makes me feel great knowing I potentially changed someone's life after buying their product. That's amazing."
- "Was just sitting here, in my heated, brick house, sipping a coffee, feeling sorry for myself as I'm in the middle of a 'rough' period, and I come across this. Thanks, Dan. Nothing like a bit of perspective to sort you out. Will buy a Sawyer on principle now."
- "What they do is a genuinely humane thing. It should be considered normal and desirable thing to do by everyone regardless of religion you subscribe to, if everyone would do something like this the World would be a much better place."

This is just a fraction of the comments. Comments like "I never knew Sawyer did projects like that" really jump out at me. We didn't spend a penny on that video. We just did what we always do by trying to help people get access to clean water. But with one social media post with no marketing dollars, we suddenly had a whole new set of people joining our loyal base, from both the tire kickers and the fringe. *This* is the power of social media. It makes it easy to tell your story and to get those casual tire kickers to take the next step without any external acquisition cost. We could've spent a lot of money on advertising to try and get those people, whereas social media basically made it free.

I worked for the power tool manufacturer SKIL in the 1980s, long before social media came along. Back then I always spent money on publicity instead of advertising. Ad dollars were a waste of time unless you were big or could localize your ads. But there was too much clutter for SKIL and print pieces lasted longer than commercials on TV. Print would stick around for a while after the commercials disappeared. And a review written by somebody else had a lot more credibility than an ad (similar to an influencer making a video today).

The value of print became social media for us. The publicity potential on social media, as we saw with Dan Becker's videos, is priceless. It can move customers from one circle to the next at little to no cost when compared to the cost of advertising. (With social media outlets constantly changing at the whim of younger generations, our team works hard to stay abreast of what each new generation is using.)

Of course, this kind of good PR is much more likely to happen if you're not just selling products but if you're out changing the world too. So, what is your organization doing?

Provide a Service, Not Just a Product

Back when we were first building our loyal base, back before we even had a full understanding of The Circle of Customers, we focused on the tried-and-true model of offering an excellent product and incredible service. No one else was manufacturing sunscreen, repellents, Extractor™ Pump Kits, and other products on the same level as ours. We may have been more expensive than some brands, but our products were based on the best science of the day. Additionally, we built a reputation with our customers for great service.

I remember a particular phone call from a longtime buyer at the now-closed Sportsmart (it merged with The Sports Authority in 2003). There were some tough things going on in the industry at the time, and the buyer called me up and said, "I can call you because I know I will always get the answer. I can't call [a competitor] because they'll never give me an answer. I don't even know who to talk to there. But I know Sawyer will always talk to me." Well, that's the difference. Our retailers knew that when they called they would actually get to talk with me or someone on my team. They knew we would give them the answer, or find the answer if we didn't know it. That was part of the service we provided. Not just the product.

We try to do one major philanthropic project each year. In 2023, we worked with The Bucket Ministry to bring clean water to Ciudad Victoria, a city in the northeast of Mexico that is home to nearly 350,000 people. In 2024, we plan to return to Kenya and begin bringing water filters into another slum close to the one in Kibera.

But we do a lot more than simply donate water filters. Again, we provide a service, not just a product. Whenever we take on a large project, we create a proposal for the nonprofit partner that outlines all the services we offer. Projects like the one Dan Becker filmed in Kibera often include:

- QR codes on every filter
  - Each filter has a unique QR code that allows our partners to monitor how the filters are being used and to track them using GIS.
  - The QR codes also provide local trainers, as well as the filter users, with access to training videos in multiple languages. They can access these videos with a phone and learn about how to install their filter, maintain it, and other best practices.

- Quality assessments of the source water, paying special attention to "forever chemicals"
- WASH training, a comprehensive training for every end user

There are no Sawyer teams that move into a remote village, set everything up, and leave. Our process has always been to train local leaders on how to install, clean, and maintain water filters so they can, in turn, train the end user. We work through local NGOs to distribute the filters, and we follow up on the status of each filter through GIS tracking.

Providing a service and not just a product can be the difference for any business or nonprofit. It is one of the things that has made Sawyer unique. I've heard customers say out loud, "Why would you use anybody but Sawyer? Somebody else might offer you a (lower quality) filter for $3 less, but they can't do what Sawyer does."

> **Providing a service and not just a product can be the difference for any business or nonprofit.**

Whether you're a customer at Amazon or an NGO in Nairobi, we're not just providing water filters and repellents; we're providing the whole package.

Loyalty Works Both Ways

It's helpful to be aware of which brands and organizations you are a loyal customer to and why. This can inform your decisions at your organization or just in your life. Be aware of whom you're supporting. Think through where you fall on their Circle of Customers. This can save you money and open up opportunities for making a greater impact around the world.

For instance, right now Sawyer is part of the loyal base for our supplier of picaridin, the primary chemical in picaridin insect repellent. If we need something, they'll almost always find a way to get it for us. Because we continue to buy from the same distributor, they take care of us when the supply is short. We get preference because we're in their loyal base. They offer us good deals because we are loyal customers. They understand that it's less costly for them to work with Sawyer on picaridin than it is for them to find new customers. It's good for us to know this because we can then make strategic requests, which in turn allows Sawyer to grow our business.

Sawyer wouldn't have survived the early days if we were part of the loyal base of three specific companies. Consolidated Press, NCL, and Communigraphics supported us all the way through the early, tough years. They did this by understanding how our business worked. They knew we needed their products in March, but that we wouldn't have the money to pay for them until August. They would wait for payment, and they didn't want any interest because they understood how the margins worked. They knew they were better off making the money than worrying about the little bit of interest.

But we always gave them the interest anyways. We wanted Sawyer to survive. They were a great source of capital. We wouldn't have been around without their support.

But, by the same token, look at it from their point of view. They were selling more to their loyal base. We were cheap. They didn't have to go out and find another customer. They had us and we would just keep buying more and more stuff from them. So, it worked both ways. We were in their loyal base, so they kept selling us more services. And because they were part of our loyal base, we kept returning to them and received the best deals and services available.

A similar, mutual partnership can take place in charitable and philanthropic efforts too. For instance, we like The Bucket Ministry. We're part of their loyal base. We like how they present their work. We like how they manage it. We like how efficient they are. We choose them. I've mentioned already that at Sawyer we try to do one major philanthropic project every year. Sometimes we'll have two hundred or more charities to choose from. We will often choose someone we know, like The Bucket Ministry.

Chapter Eight

Turning Your Customers into Partners

Years and years ago, we had the Extractor™ Pump Kit at Walmart. At the time, we shipped them in case packs of six kits because Walmart's fourteen-inch peg held six kits. One day, I sat down with the buyer and she said, "You don't have an 80 percent in-stock rating." That meant that 20 percent of the time the peg was empty. Empty pegs mean the retailer is losing money, the manufacturer is losing money, and the end consumer isn't getting the product they need. So, I changed the case pack from six to four. Sales of the Extractor™ Pump Kit went up 20 percent at Walmart. The next four-pack would show up while there were still two on the peg. Then they would restock the kits out to the end again. The peg never ran empty and sales increased. All I had to do was pay another three cents per unit for the new box.

This was an epiphany for me! This experience motivated me to begin using a concept called Gross Margin Return on Investment, or GMROI (pronounced /G/IM-roy), which I still use to this day. I realized it was in both Sawyer's interest and our retail partner's interest to keep those shelves full by shipping in case packs that would not allow them to run out but also did not give them so many that they had a surplus.

At Sawyer, we will take the same product and put it in two packs, four packs, eight packs, or twelve packs, all depending on which trade partner the case is going to.

This drives manufacturing nuts. They would rather package every product in a case of forty-eight! They don't want to have to stock all the different case-quantity boxes. But I'm more interested in having the store maximize their profit per cubic inch by never having excess inventory there and never running out either.

At Sawyer, we often say that "the most expensive packaging is the one that doesn't sell." Offering multiple case pack sizes might increase our cost by a few cents per unit, but as long as the case packs are rolling out the door, the volume is worth the cost.

At Walmart and some other retailers, surplus units are stuck up above the shelf. Those units are easy to forget about. Meanwhile, the computer still says they're in inventory. So, a consumer could be looking at an empty peg while the computer says the retailer still has two in stock and won't automatically reorder more. This could go on for days, or weeks in some cases, until someone finds the surplus above the shelf. (Next time you're in Walmart, take a look at the products sitting on that top shelf. It's probably a little of this and a little that which they couldn't fit on the pegs.) Not every retailer will do that. Some will leave surplus inventory in the back of the warehouse where it is forgotten about. Wherever the retailer stashes the surplus, their computer won't forget it's there. The computer will show that they have one or two products in stock, even when the peg is empty, and then reorders get missed

Situations like these don't do us any good, they don't do the retailer any good, and they don't do the consumer any good. If the consumer is looking for something and they can't find it in the store, then they're going to go somewhere else to find it. Or they might not take the time to find it at all and buy an alternative instead.

Using GMROIs has taught us that adjusting our case pack to match any given retailer's needs will allow us to hit the sweet spot where everybody's happy, including the CFOs.

The purpose of GMROI is to *maximize your retailer's profit*. This may seem like an odd way to think about running your business. Shouldn't you focus on your own profits? Or, perhaps focus on what consumer needs are? Why spend time and energy on helping your retailers increase their profits? That's for them to do.

These are natural questions. However, I've learned that focusing on GMROI will not only maximize retailer profits but ultimately serve you and the end consumer better too. It's a win-win-win that helped Sawyer disrupt the water filter market.[30]

---

[30] In the years since Walmart has told us we have an 80 percent in-stock rating, our in-stock rating has climbed to 99 percent. We try to be a great partner and never let those pegs sit empty. Keep it turning.

What Is a GMROI?

The basic formula for determining the Gross Margin Return on Investment is as follows:

$$\frac{(A - B) \times C}{B \times D \times E}$$

A = Retail price
B = The retailer's landed cost
C = The number of units sold that year on that peg
D = The number of units in the pipeline (on the peg, in the warehouse, in transit) which represents the retailer's total investment
E = The footprint of your product, the cubic space it takes up in the retail store. We will use just one for this simple analysis. Later in the chapter, we'll discuss more complex ways to calculate E.

If you can't figure out all the various costs in B (the freight, the breakbulk, the insurance, etc.), then for the purposes of GMROI, you can just assume it's 10 percent above your selling price. If you're in a different industry, such as grocery, you'd use more than 10 percent. If you're in seasonal apparel, you might also use a higher percentage due to the extra clothing you need to sell off at the end of a season. But if you're selling hard goods that don't expire or spoil (it's not fashion that goes out of style or food that spoils), then you can simply use 10 percent. This is Math Trap working for you. It doesn't really matter if it's 8 percent or 10 percent or whatever it may be because the answer isn't going to change dramatically, and your resulting decision won't change.

The numerator in this equation represents the amount of profit margin generated by that peg for the year. The denominator is the retailer's full investment.

As a manufacturer and marketer, my questions are: How can I help the retail buyer meet his or her goals? How can I turn them into a partner? How can Sawyer help each retailer succeed?

The Retail Buyer's World

In this section, I'm going to talk about Sawyer's relationships in a retail environment. But these principles apply to restaurants, services, insurance, etc. These concepts apply to any business you may be in.

For many retailers, you can assume that 90 percent of their sales come from 30 to 40 percent of their items. The rest are there to create an image that they have a full department of whatever type of products they're attempting to sell, e.g., a camping department, a home department, a toy department, etc. This is because of a concept called *full line*. Full line means that if you want to have a camping department, you can't just stock the bestselling items. You also have to stock the popcorn poppers and glow sticks and all the little gadgets that don't justify space on their own, but, when seen together, they create the image of a camping department for the consumer. Full line purchases are meant to shape the perception of the end consumer, allowing retailers to be perceived the way they want to be.

Retailers know which pegs hold their bestselling items and which ones hold the products that are there to fill out the department and hopefully make some money too. (Take a look at the next camping department you walk into. There's no way the soap bar holders are making as much on their pegs as the truly hot items are.) A safe estimate, based on profit per peg, is that around 30 percent of a given department would not justify its space on a peg. But retailers wouldn't get anybody to walk down the aisle if they cherrypicked only the bestselling items.

Understanding full line helped us sell the Extractor™ Pump Kit in the early days because you couldn't have a camping department without a snake bite kit.

I learned another valuable lesson about retail before I started Sawyer while I was at SKIL. It's a sound marketing concept called *good, better, best*. This is about having three layers of products and using products one and three to sell product two. First, we had a basic circular saw—a *good* product. Then we had one that was a little *better*. It didn't cost us much to make it better, but it was truly better. Then we had the super-duper one which was the *best* product in our line. Most consumers weren't going to buy it, though, because of the cost. But that was OK. The good saw and the best saw were there in order to sell the better saw, which is the one we really wanted people to purchase. It was where our profits were.

It's a marketing strategy that works well to this day. Your retail partners are probably aware of it, so you should be too. If you're a manufacturer, then it may be wise to begin offering three variations of the same product. You want retailers and consumers to buy the middle one. Insurance companies have this down to a science. "We have our golden policies. We have our basic program . . . ." And then they have the one you should actually buy.

Whatever the retailer, do your homework and understand the concepts that make an impact on their work. Understanding full line, employing *good, better, best*, and knowing which pegs hold the bestselling items are just the first steps into the retailer's world.

Understanding Your Retailer's Numerator

In Chapter Four, we discussed Math Trap and learned that understanding the relationship between the numerator and the denominator is fundamental to strategic thinking. This understanding allows you to get to good business decisions quickly and develop correct strategies without knowing all the details. Math Trap comes into play again as we consider the next steps into a retail buyer's world.

In most retail settings, the buyer typically focuses on the numerator. They are primarily concerned with how much money they can make for each widget they sell. In order to increase their profits, they'll challenge the supplier on cost, they'll get promotional dollars, and they'll try all kinds of ways to increase their margins. This focus—the money made on the sale of each widget—is their numerator.

The problem is that the numerator is pretty hard to move. Buyers can't push back against their vendors too much. They don't want to damage the relationship. They can try to grow sales, but there are always challenges there. So, profits are made in the denominator because growing sales is really not as important as managing your investment wisely. Remember our discussion about Walmart's success? They beat everybody by managing their investment, which reduced their denominator.

This is usually understood by someone in the finance department at the retailer's corporate office. It's not uncommon for corporate offices to give their buyers a purchasing plan called *open-to-buy*. Essentially, the finance department tells a buyer, "You can spend X amount this week or this month and that's all. You can't spend any more than that." It's the responsibility of the retail buyer to then figure out how to meet their sales goals and get the most return with those dollars.

Buyers in these situations can't have everything they want. This leads to empty pegs. In order to achieve their sales goals, buyers shift their focus to only the bestselling items—not necessarily the items with the highest margins, but the items with the highest number of turns.

It's helpful to ask yourself at this point: Is my company's product a bestselling item? Or is it purchased in order to help retailers have a full line? If your product is often purchased because of a full-line strategy, then you may end up without reorders—empty pegs—if the retail buyer is shifted to an open-to-buy purchasing plan. (Remember, empty pegs aren't good for anyone.)

Open-to-buy is one form of GMROI management. The finance department uses open-to-buy to manage the buyers and increase the gross margin return on their investments. They may not be able to afford full-line purchases when interest rates are high or when they have restricted capital. Open-to-buy is a technique they'll use to force the buyers into maximizing their GMROIs.

Another way to think about this is to remember that many retail buyers get their bonuses based on how much money they make for the company. They know they'll make the most money on items that turn regularly. The higher the number of turns, the more likely they are to reach their sales objectives. Open-to-buy doesn't force them to make certain margins but rather to reach sales objectives, e.g., number of turns. So again, the retail buyer ends up focusing on the bestselling items, not the highest-margin items. They invest less (the denominator) to get more out of the numerator. This is GMROI in action.

Let's take a deeper look at what comprises the retailer's numerator. Here's a typical list of costs to the retailer in order to sell each product. There could be up to thirty or more specific costs depending on the retailer and their circumstances.

- Cost of the product
- Freight
- Breaking bulk (breaking down the pallets at the warehouse, stocking shelves with individual units, etc.)
- Insurance
- Financing
- Real estate
- Promotions
- Shrink (typically theft) or spillage

Every one of these costs are in the retailer's numerator (represented above as variable B). They've purchased the product, but somebody's got to pay for the freight. Somebody's got to take the freight and break it down from a pallet to a box to the stuff on the shelf. Then there's the necessary insurance and financing. They have to pay for their building, their promotions, and also eat the shrink.[31]

---

31 Shrink includes theft. It can also include messy scenarios like "Cleanup in aisle 4" or products used to give out samples (like free food samples). Shrink occurs with commodities such as gasoline too. A tanker fills the tank with 10,000 gallons, but because of evaporation, only 9,600 gallons make it to the station. Shrink can also occur anytime items are bought from a vat (like peanuts or flour).

The result (A − B) is called the store's *net profit*. Whenever a retailer puts any product on the shelf, they've already calculated all those costs. They had to pay for all that stuff in order to put your product on their peg.

Margins are calculated by this formula: $((A - B) \div A)$.

Finance departments will often give retail buyers directives like, "You've got to work on getting a 30 percent margin," or, "You've got to work on the 40 percent margin," or sometimes even, "You need to get 55 percent margins on everything you sell." They give them these targets so the company can absorb all those costs that make up overhead. Those costs are not usually measured product by product, but they don't go away either. Imagine a retail buyer sells something for $10. They know they bought it for $5 and so the buyer thinks they've made a 50 percent margin. But the company knows they need buyers to make 50 percent margins because the overhead might take up 10 percent or more of that 50 percent. So, the finance department knows they're only making 40 percent.

That's how the game works. Some retail buyers know this, but some don't. Some will know to factor in more than just freight when they're calculating how much they've paid for a product, but not all of them will. Regardless, that's how the corporate office measures the numerator, and it's good for you to know so you can best maximize your retailer's profit.

Understanding Your Retailer's Denominator

In 2023, a major camping and hiking retail chain cut its denominator in half by letting its inventory pipeline go empty. They made this decision because interest rates were so high. (They weren't the only retailer to do so. Everybody seemed to be trying to aggressively manage their inventories.) The strategy was called *go narrow, go deep*. Instead of offering three or four options for every need, they limited their selections to two. It would be like visiting a grocery store and expecting to find umpteen brands of cornflakes in the cereal aisle but only finding a couple. This strategy opened up space for other products without losing many sales, making up the profits with something else in that space.

For this retailer, bicycles became hot items during and after the Covid-19 pandemic. They "narrowed" the selection and space in many adjacent departments to make room for more bikes. In Sawyer's case, the narrower line helped us as we gained more focus from customers. The water products category got decluttered, which was to our favor. Sawyer water filter sales went up 16 percent despite a 40 percent SKU reduction in this retailer's camping department. They got a GMROI boost through less investment in water products and space without losing net sales *and* they sold more bikes.

But wouldn't this strategy also cause them to lose sales on other hot items? No, it just meant they would have to reorder more often. By keeping their inventory down, they avoided paying the high interest rate.

No retailer can let the pipeline run completely empty. It has to be kept up to satisfy consumers. So, either they're going to put more inventory back in—probably not because of the interest rates—or they're going to order more often and just keep rolling the products through. Sometimes this is called *just-in-time* ordering.

In addition to this change in investment, many retailers responded to high interest rates by taking high-priced items out of their stores, including some Sawyer products. Because the buyer is focused on the denominator, they took out anything that wasn't turning quickly enough and decided to just let consumers buy those items online.

The high interest rates of 2023 revealed a basic concept in action: *the greatest way to improve your return on investment is to cut your investment,* i.e., your denominator.

Understanding your retail partner's denominator is a little more complex than their numerator because it represents their full investment. This investment is paid for out of the margins. Imagine that you're the CFO of a major retailer and you're looking at all the costs required for you to invest in products. You have to sweep the floor at night, run the cash registers, advertise, pay for all the equipment, pay for the shelves, etc. All of that is yours to cover. That's your denominator.

The Cost of Every Peg

Next time you walk into a Walmart, REI, Dick's Sporting Goods, or any other retailer, take a look around and think about how many pegs you see. Many retail chains know—or at least try to determine—exactly how much profit they make off of every peg in their store. They ask themselves: How many times do we sell that product divided by the cost of that space? Most retailers will be able to tell you what every peg costs. It's a cubic calculation. Let me give you an example from Sawyer's history.

If you were injured out in the wilderness, three hours or three days away from help, what would you need in a first aid kit other than a bunch of bandages you get from many basic kits?

Back in the '80s, everyone said things like "put on a bandage" and head to the ER. Nobody knew what to do when you fell down the side of the mountain and help couldn't get there for hours, or you were days away and they had to use a helicopter to get you out. That's all different from today, but those were the '80s.

We were big in first aid at the time and helped invent what's called wilderness first aid. It's a product that answers this question: What do you do if you're three hours or three days away from medical help?

The group developed ways to treat hypothermia, frostbite, and heat exhaustion. Many of our ideas actually came from the military asking us, "What do we do if our injured soldiers are remote?" So, we built a first aid kit to address all those things. It wasn't just a bunch of bandages. It had things you could really use for emergency medical care, along with an appropriate number of bandages.

Our product included a manual, which basically taught the average consumer triage. It was phenomenal and became an industry standard. It taught people how to quickly analyze an injury like an EMT and then walked them through emergency treatment. We ended up making seven different sizes, meeting the needs of consumers who might just be on a little day hike as well as those who would be out in the wilderness for much longer.

Our wilderness first aid kit was a great product, but unfortunately Sawyer is not in that market much anymore. Another buyer came in and said, "You've only got fifty-six items in your kit while this one's got one hundred and ten."

I replied, "Yeah, but sixty of them are the little three-eighths-of-an-inch bandage, which you can't use unless you prick your finger." Unfortunately, they started making decisions based on how many items were in each kit and our better product was removed from the store. (Half of those items are truly not useful. One competitor might say "a count of 110," but consumers could do ten times more with our count of fifty than they could do with 110 simple bandages.)

Before we moved out of that market, we went to our Walmart buyer and put our kit on one of their pegs. We were quickly told that it was too big. Our kit was maybe seven inches by twelve inches—nice and thin so you could put a lot on the shelf. The buyer told us, "If you could take three inches off that, I'll put it in the store."

So, we took the header and brought it down partly over the kit. Now the product hung seven inches by nine inches. This gave the buyer twenty-one square inches of peg space to sell something else with and he stocked our kits! Freeing up that peg space was the difference between selling him $1 million of a wilderness first aid kit that can truly help those far away from medical care and selling him $0. He didn't want to invest that peg space in our larger packaging footprint. But after repackaging the same product to maximize their peg space, we made a significant sale.

I always try to focus on the lowest system cost from our factory to the end consumer. How can we work with the retailer to make that as low as possible? What function can we perform cheaper than them?

That's GMROI in action. That's how we could help our retail partner maximize their profits.

Here's another story that demonstrates how retailers think. For a few years, Sawyer water filters sold very well to retailers that attracted well-informed consumers who sought out high-performance products. We maintained the Sawyer Standard on every filter we produced.[32] Things were going well for these high-performance filters. Then I learned that one of our retail partners, a major hiking and camping store, was planning to remove Sawyer water filters and replace them with a competing filter that was an inferior product. People were buying it at the time because it had a name on it and the competitor did a lot of promotion, but you couldn't really use the filter itself. It didn't even work. But they sold, usually to this retailer's customers who were typically quite knowledgeable.

I spoke with the buyer and said, "You're going to walk away from the market, from the filter that really does work, and people come into your store looking for it, just to sell this impulse thing that doesn't work? They're only buying it 'just in case there's a disaster' (as it said on the packaging). But they're going to be sorely disappointed when the disaster shows up and they find out they can't use it."

The buyer told me, "I sell a million dollars' worth of that filter each year. If I took that out, I'd get fired."

"But it doesn't work!" I said.

"I know it doesn't work, but I sold a million dollars' worth."

As disappointing as this story may be, I didn't think ill of that buyer. He understood two things well: (1) the cost of every

---

[32] Every Sawyer water filter is 100 percent individually tested three times, not batch tested. Every filter is ~75 percent stronger than fibers of other typical hollow-fiber membranes. Every filter has an absolute pore size of 0.1 microns, meaning not a single pore is larger than 0.1 microns. This is the Sawyer Standard for water filters. It is totally unmatched.

peg in his store; (2) where he is on the bell curve. He understood his niche of customers. It was up to me and the team at Sawyer to figure out how to work with *him*, serve *his niche*, and to maximize both his profit and ours.

The question to ask yourself again is: Where am I on the bell curve? Where is my customer? How can I make sure that every peg that holds our products is highly profitable?

Anytime you can make your retail partner more money per square inch or cubic inch it's to your benefit, even if you suffer a higher cost. The Walmart story at the beginning of this chapter is a perfect example. Sales went up 20 percent because we added three cents to the cost on something for which we made good margins.

(In the GMROI equation, $B \times D \times E$ makes up the denominator. At the beginning of the chapter, I suggested just using E to represent your product's footprint and that $E = 1$. For a more complex analysis, you can make $E = $ length $\times$ width of the peg space for your product. You can even make $E = $ length $\times$ width $\times$ depth. You may not have all of this information at first, but you may be able to get it from your retail partner over time.)

If you know what situations your retail partner is facing, then before you even go into the meeting, you can adjust your packaging or your presentation to focus on helping that partner get more turns on your peg.

One idea is to use a just-in-time management method. We used to ship to some retailers directly from our warehouse. Now we ship to them every day via a supplier, which helps them with their turns of our products. This is another way we can be a good partner. Retailers need good partners. They have to have good suppliers. Just as you're looking for a good partner, they are looking for a good partner, and you're solving problems together. Being a hero to your retail partners is never a bad thing.

Understand How Your Retailer Thinks

There's an old fable about a scorpion and a frog. The scorpion wants to cross a river but it cannot swim, so it asks the frog for a ride. The frog hesitates, knowing a scorpion's sting could kill it. The scorpion reasons, "Why would I sting you? Then we would both drown." But sure enough, halfway across the river, the scorpion stings the frog. Before they both meet their demise, the frog asks why. "Because I am a scorpion" is the response.

The point of this fable is that you can't ask people to change their nature. Though this is a grisly fable, it's a good lesson to keep in mind when dealing with a retail buyer. Retail buyers love to say no. Because if she doesn't say no, she's not a buyer! That's what buyers do. So, what do you do as a vendor who is trying to build a solid partnership?

Always give the retail buyer *a reason* to say no.

This might seem like bad advice, but it's a tactic I learned early on that has helped me a great deal over the years. I would open up meetings with a presentation of a product she could reject. Buyers are protecting their company when they say no. So, never give them the best thing first. Show them what you really want them to buy second or third. Then you're more likely to hear, "No, I can't buy that, but I can buy this."

Frogs and scorpions aside, it's essential for anyone in business to understand how your retail partner thinks. Walmart thinks differently than Bass Pro. REI thinks differently than Tractor Supply. They all think differently from one another. I don't care what product you're selling; you need to understand how they think.

For years I've told the team at Sawyer, "Don't even think about going into a presentation until you have pretended you're on the receiving side of the desk. Understand what the buyer has to do."

- Does she have to come up with co-op dollars?
- Is he being managed by ad dollars?
- Does she need freight allowances?
- What are the pressures he's facing in the current season?
- What are her goals and measurements for success?

Do everything you can to understand your retail partners. Sit on their side of the desk and learn about the challenges they face.

> **Sit on your partner's side of the desk and understand the challenges they face.**

One of the ways we do this is to hire independent sales reps. In most cases, I prefer to have a rep that's more loyal to a retailer like Dick's or Bass Pro than they are to Sawyer. These reps make a living off of their specific retailer and because they do, they've truly learned all that they can about that retailer. Someone with that kind of knowledge is who I want representing Sawyer products to the buyer. Someone who truly understands what it's like to be on the buyer's side of the desk is someone who can effectively represent the retailer to us.

Your retail partners are not the only people to understand, of course. You also need to understand your retailers' customers—the end consumers. Each retailer will have different types of consumers. You need to factor all that in.

Start by going where you'll be most successful. For example, Sawyer Products are not in drugstores. We've explored it, but we've learned that the person going to the drugstore isn't focused on high-performance products or even brand shopping. If they're a parent with a carload of kids on a road trip, they won't really give a rip about the brand of sunscreen. They just need something right away and they're going to buy it. They are not going to stand around and look at which of the two sunscreens is better. They're just making sure to buy a new bottle for that carload of kids.

So, you need to understand your end consumer, but you also need to understand anything between your end consumer and you. Take the time to sit on the other side of the desk and understand your retail partner first, then take the time to understand your retailer's unique customers, the end consumer. We spend a lot of time in retail stores listening to the end consumer.

One of Our Partner's Stories: The Old Man in Fiji

There was an old man in Fiji who had a cough for nineteen years. This may sound like the beginning of another fable, but this story is as real as the global water crisis. Doctors couldn't figure out why his cough continued for so long. Nothing they offered him seemed to make a difference. No treatment worked. In 2014, he was given a Sawyer International Bucket System by a nonprofit ministry called Give Clean Water, which was founded by Darrel Larson.

During an eight-week follow-up visit, Darrel and his team learned that the man's cough was gone. A nineteen-year untreatable ailment just vanished. Because of clean water? Why? How?

The answer is sediment. The dictionary defines sediment as "the matter that settles to the bottom of a liquid" and "material deposited by water, wind, or glaciers."[33] This definition, while accurate, is too benign for the devastating effects of sediment on the human body. Sediment is like sandpaper on the throat. It is gritty and can coat the esophagus the way primer seals a wall.

In Fiji, as in many other places around the world, people frequently get their water from open wells. They often dig these wells themselves. Sometimes they simply bore holes in the ground or dig a large pit to find water, but it is rarely clean water. The water they find is often as dark as Coca-Cola, turbid with sediment and granularities. Every fresh rainfall stirs up the water into a new, cloudy mess.

By using the Bucket System, the man was able to remove sediment from his drinking water. His esophagus was no longer subject to daily coats of grime and the cough disappeared. The Give Clean Water team was thrilled to learn of this man's recovery, and I was equally thrilled to hear about it later. In just eight weeks, he was completely healed of something he'd battled for nearly twenty years!

Darrel and his team also learned that, for everyone using Sawyer water filters, diarrhea rates in the same area had declined steeply. This data-gathering approach would eventually lead to big things at Sawyer and even bigger things around the world. Not only would Darrel join our staff as International Director,

---

[33] "Sediment," Merriam-Webster, accessed January 11, 2024, https://www.merriam-webster.com/dictionary/sediment.

but data-gathering would become a critical part of how we tackle the global water crisis. As I've said already, tracking numbers and making sense of ROI is intrinsic to my thinking. This story and hundreds like it showed me and the others at Sawyer what kind of ROI—in the form of real lives being changed—we could get with the water filters. Profit is a wonderful ROI. But curing a man of a chronic cough? That kind of ROI is invaluable.

There was an old man in Fiji who had a cough for nineteen years. Now he does not. This is no fable. This is a real life changed.

Chapter Nine

Protecting Your Business for Future Growth

Businesses fail all the time. We've all heard people say that half of all businesses fail. *Forbes Advisor* puts a finer point on this old adage and reports that 20 percent of small businesses fail in the first year, 30 percent will fail in the second year, and a total of 50 percent will fail by year five.[34] Naturally, none of us want our business to be included in one of those statistics. So, what can be done? In this chapter, we're going to talk about different ways to analyze and protect your business. We're going to discuss various tidbits of wisdom that have cemented into a solid foundation for me over the years.

It's important to note that when I use the word *protect* in this chapter it has more than one meaning. Protecting your business,

---

34 Kelly Main and Cassie Bottorff, "Small Business Statistics Of 2024," *Forbes Advisor*, updated January 31, 2024, https://www.forbes.com/advisor/business/small-business-statistics/#small_business_survival_statistics_section.

of course, means that you prevent people from trying to undercut you or steal from you. But protecting your business isn't just about being attacked. It's also about protecting your profitability. As I've said, we can't know the future, but we can practice future thinking. (Remember, one of the fundamental ideas within Creative Destruction is that *things are going to change*.) Future thinking is what will lead to greater success. Future thinking is what leads us to growth. This chapter, then, is about protecting that future by analyzing and protecting your business today.

Patents

Many people assume that as soon as you create something new, you should get it patented. That's an understandable conclusion; however, let's consider an argument for why you should (sometimes) *not* get a patent.

There are three types of US patents—utility, design, and plant. Since Sawyer is primarily concerned with the creation and marketing of manufactured products, our experience has been with utility and design patents.[35] The US Patent Office says utility patents are for "inventing a new or improved and useful process, machine, article of manufacture, or composition of matter" while design patents are for "inventing a new, original, and ornamental design for an article of manufacture."[36]

Before you apply for either of these patents, you need to ask yourself: *Is the patent going to protect my business, or is the*

---

35 If you're in the business of inventing or cultivating new varieties of plants, visit https://www.uspto.gov/patents/basics/apply for more information about plant patents.
36 "Patent Essentials," United States Patent and Trademark Office, accessed January 8, 2024, https://www.uspto.gov/patents/basics/essentials#questions.

patent going to disclose so much information that my competitors will be able to design around my product?* This is the danger with filing for a patent. The process requires you to disclose how you made your product. That information then becomes public record, and interested parties, like your competitors, can review that information to their heart's content and design around it; it's called reverse engineering.

Filing for a patent is like giving away a secret recipe. It's helping your competitor's R&D and engineering people go down the learning curve very quickly. They may not know how your new widget works. But once the patent is issued, they can study your product/formula/design/etc. and simply change their product a little bit to get around the patent. In most cases, we have not applied for patents of Sawyer products because we don't want our competitors to know what we're doing.

Besides giving away your secret recipe, patents need to be defended in court if they are violated. That burden—the time and the costs associated with litigation—*falls to the patent holder*. If you're a relatively small or independent company that has disrupted an established market with a new, patented product, then it will be on your dime to take the big companies to court when they start copying you.

Imagine that you're a small, upstart company that has created a new insect repellent. It's not DEET. It's not picaridin. It's not anything that's been done before. It's totally new and it's taking the insect repellent market by storm. But as good as your new product is, it's not rocket science. The big brands quickly assign a team to figure out the "recipe" (or a close proximity) so they can release their own version. Sure enough, the big brands release their version and it starts to take customers from you. You begin to lose significant profit and your business starts to suffer.

If you have patented the recipe, and if you believe they've copied it, then *you* will have to hire a lawyer and take on those big brands in court. You can bet that each of those big brands will have umpteen lawyers and very deep pockets to pay those lawyers for as long as it takes to win the case. You might own the patent on the recipe, but defending the patent in court against opponents like those would simply not be feasible.

In many cases, even if you could win the court case, the penalty the big brands would have to pay is so minimal (relative to the size of their business) that they'll simply pay it and move on, probably designing around your patent or even violating it again.

To put the cost of patent litigation in perspective, here are some quick stats from the technology research and forensic firm Copperpod Intellectual Property:[37]

Patent Litigation Statistics in General

- Each year, between 5,000 and 6,000 patent cases are filed in the United States.
- Patent applications increased by 4 percent in 2020, despite the COVID-19 epidemic.
- During the year 2020, US courts awarded $4.67 billion in patent damages.
- Patent litigation costs between $2.3 million and $4 million on average.

---

37 "How Much Does Patent Litigation Cost?," Copperpod Intellectual Property, May 11, 2022, https://www.copperpodip.com/post/how-much-does-patent-litigation-cost.

- It takes one to three years for a patent case to reach trial. [I would add that, during this period of time, the violator continues to sell and grab market share.]
- Patent infringement lawsuits are settled in 95 percent to 97 percent of cases.

As you can see from this list, defending a patent in court can be a very costly and time-consuming process. A real-life example of the cost of patent litigation and the power of big brands with big teams of attorneys is the story of Robert Kearns. Kearns designed and patented intermittent windshield wipers. Your car has an intermittent windshield wiper design. Your wipers intermittently wipe the windshield clean at different speeds. Before Kearns's innovation, wipers only moved continuously at either fast or slow speeds. You can imagine how unpleasant it might have been to drive with wipers like that. Kearns created wiper blades to work intermittently because he wanted wipers to "blink" the way a human eye does. The large auto companies were so impressed by his design that they quickly began producing cars with intermittent wiper blades, which sent Kearns into a long court battle with them. He was ultimately awarded $20 million and is considered a hero—a David who took down corporate goliaths. But the court battles lasted for decades and were incredibly costly.[38]

As inspiring as Kearns's story is (it was even made into a Hollywood movie, *Flash of Genius*), it is an outlier. Most patent

---

38 Dan Morrell, "Blink of An Eye: The Accidental Birth of a Standard Auto Feature," Think, Case Western Reserve University, accessed January 8, 2024, https://case.edu/think/fall2016/blink-of-eye.html#:~:text=Robert%20Kearns%2C%20PhD%20(CIT%20',leaving%20him%20with%20impaired%20vision.

holders are not successful at winning court cases against big companies. They usually get stampeded. So, a good rule of thumb is, *if someone can probably design around your product, don't file for a patent.* Don't share your secret recipe. Make your competitors work to figure it out.

When should you apply for a patent? Is it ever wise to do so?

I think it's wise to apply for a patent only when you think the odds are pretty small that your competitors can design around it. If it is easy to design around your product, then the patent is of little value. Also, consider applying for a patent only if you think you'll be able to defend it in court if a large company tries to openly violate your patent (as the auto companies did to Robert Kearns).

People tend to think of patents as protection for their ideas. And they are, to a point. They legally establish who created what. But while a patent may protect who gets the credit for an innovation, they do not necessarily protect your business. There are no patent police that will jump in for you when your patent is violated. Your business could suffer significantly even if you hold a patent, and perhaps even *because* you hold the patent and revealed your secret recipe.

Protecting a patent means that it's on you to sue anyone violating that patent. It may not be worth the time and money to do so.

On the positive side, some retailers and Amazon may be hesitant to add a potential violator because they don't want to get involved in the litigation. Thus, you can create a trade barrier even with a weak patent.

Invest in Brand Equity and Trade Equity

In 1988, RJR Nabisco Inc. (better known to consumers as simply "Nabisco") accepted a buyout from the Wall Street investment firm

Kohlberg Kravis Roberts & Co. (KKR) for $24.5 billion. It was a historic corporate takeover still studied in MBA programs today. Why did KKR buy Nabisco? Because of their brand equity.[39]

Brand equity is all about your relationship with the end consumer. It's the commercial value of your brand based on the consumer's perception of your brand name. KKR wanted Nabisco because it had strong brand equity in grocery stores. Nabisco products included Ritz, Triscuits, Lifesavers, Baby Ruth and Butterfinger candy bars, Planters Peanuts, Animal Crackers, Oreo cookies and countless other products that you instantly recognize and are likely to have a positive association with. For example, if someone asks you to pick up a can of peanuts on the way to a Super Bowl party, you are likely to grab a jar of Planters Peanuts, even if you rarely eat peanuts yourself, because you trust that Planters Peanuts are what your friends will like. A sizable segment of the market will pay a premium for a major brand name over brand X or a lesser brand. That is brand equity.

Sawyer has been careful to build our brand equity in specific channels of distribution. Going back to the bell curve (see Chapter One), we know who our customers are and where they shop. We reach early educators and early innovators with our high-performance products. In certain channels of distribution—like a dedicated hunting and camping retailer—we have incredible brand equity. For instance, consumers are willing to try new Sawyer products because they have had a great experi-

---

[39] "Nabisco Accepts Buyout Offer," Washington Post, Jerry Knight, November 30, 1988, accessed January 8, 2024, https://www.washingtonpost.com/archive/politics/1988/12/01/nabisco-accepts-buyout-offer/f314e888-476a-4a02-b167-0c1d1c2b7abc/.

ence over the last several years while hiking with their Sawyer water filter.

This is all intuitive so far, but it's also helpful to know when and where you *don't* have much brand equity. For example, the big brand producers of DEET-based insect repellent have significant brand equity in other channels of distribution. They've spent time (and billions of dollars) competing for that brand equity. In retail channels that don't primarily target the early educators and early innovators that we target—like the average Walmart, drug, and grocery stores—they have more brand equity than us. This information is useful to us because it affects our strategy (and our spending) in those channels.

So, understanding when and where you do and don't have brand equity is incredibly important for protecting your business. Understanding your brand equity not only helps you make money, but it also determines where it is best to spend money.

Trade equity is similar, but it's about the relationship you have with your retail partners rather than your consumers. Sawyer has strong trade equity with a number of major retailers. This comes from years, sometimes decades, of maintaining good relationships with these companies. For years we have worked with them on discounts, endcap displays, promotions, packaging, and anything else you can name. Most importantly, we have sent Sawyer employees out to visit retail stores in person, where they spend time educating the staff on Sawyer products. No other approach has helped build our trade equity as much as simply spending time in the stores with retail staff. Why? Because most of Sawyer's early-educator, early-innovator customers shop at customer-assisted retail stores like REI, Bass Pro, and others.

In retail settings like those, it is critical for the staff to know the products inside and out. So, our investment in sending Sawyer employees to those stores has paid huge dividends, and not just financially, but relationally.

Another significant factor in building trade equity is to ask your retail partners, "What can we do for you?" That question is gold. We once asked Walmart that question. In reply, they asked us to make bed nets and head nets for campers fighting mosquitos. The team at Sawyer turned around and made the best on the market. Bed nets and head nets are products we probably wouldn't have made if they hadn't asked. Our team tries to stay away from copycat products. But since our retailer asked for them, we made them. And we made sure to make better nets than any of the competitors. When your retailers are comfortable enough to ask you for products, you've got trade equity. But be sure to follow it up with an amazing product.

The last important piece to building trade equity almost goes without saying. You must have a product that sells. As we said in our discussion about the Four Ps of Marketing, having a product that people actually want and need is key to success. That might seem obvious, but there are a lot of people who don't get that. It is not what you think people want or need; it is what they think they want or need.

Trade equity is increasingly important. In the last ten to fifteen years, retailers have demonstrated that they don't want to work with a lot of vendors. They would prefer to write one purchase order (PO) with twenty items on it rather than twenty POs with one item. The reasons for this are obvious. Fewer POs means fewer shipments received, fewer pallets unloaded, less time breaking bulk, more efficiency in the back of the store, and all around more savings for them.

With retailers operating this way, it's pretty tough to displace a proven, solid vendor with strong trade equity, even if you have a better mousetrap. That new mousetrap has got to be a monumental improvement over the old in order for a newcomer to upset a strong relationship. So, if you want to protect your business, then spend time building trade equity and fostering the relationship with your retailers. For more specifics on how to foster those relationships, turn back to Chapter Seven, "The Circle of Customers," and Chapter Eight, "Turning Your Customers into Partners."

To Protect Your Business, Protect Your Brand

A friend of mine was traveling in Colorado. While he was there, he met a young man who had recently returned from a hiking trip in the Rockies. During their conversation, my friend asked him, "How do you make sure you have enough clean water when you're hiking through the mountains?"

"Oh, I have my Sawyer," the young man responded casually. He then described the Sawyer Squeeze Water Filtration System without actually naming it.

"He just called it, 'My Sawyer,'" my friend told me. "He didn't call it 'My Sawyer water filter' or even 'My water filter.' Just, 'My Sawyer.'"

You might think this is a good thing, a testament to our brand recognition, maybe even a statement about our brand equity, but I always cringe when I hear stories like these. For anyone managing a brand and for anyone managing a product disrupting their market, this kind of consumer behavior can be dangerous. Why? Because you need to protect your brand from becoming the default name for a category of products. When consumers name whole categories after the leading product in that category, you lose control of your own name.

For example, people say "Pass me a Kleenex," but what they're really asking for is a facial tissue. It may not actually matter to them if it's a Kleenex facial tissue or not. Any facial tissue will do. People also say, "I'd like some Jell-O for dessert." But many people don't care if it's actually brand name Jell-O gelatin or not. They just want to eat some gelatin. The same is true with Band-Aids and other products. These brands have become the generic name for a product or product category. The owners of these brands have to work hard and spend a great deal of money not to lose control of the brands they no doubt spent years (even decades) building.

Many larger companies have enough lawyers to help protect their brand by not allowing others to use their name generically. But, like filing for a patent, this work is costly, and smaller companies do not have as much clout.

Years before starting Sawyer, I worked at Weed Eater. Weed Eater's brand weakened as it became associated with the "string trimmer" category. Soon, consumers were buying "Toro weed eaters" and "Black and Decker weed eaters." The weakening brand made it difficult for Weed Eater to sell ancillary products such as hedge trimmers and lawn mowers. Because they couldn't protect their brand from becoming the default name for a whole category, they ended up losing brand equity and couldn't sell other Weed Eater brand products effectively. It was a lesson I took to heart.

To avoid weakening the Sawyer brand, we always carefully name the product category after we use the name, e.g., The Sawyer Squeeze Water Filtration System, The Sawyer Stay-Put SPF 30 Sunscreen, The Sawyer Picaridin Insect Repellent. This approach makes it more difficult to separate and associate our name with just one product.

Early on we had a brand protection issue with our flagship product, the Sawyer Extractor™ Pump Kit. Others tried the "Xtractor" or the "Brand A venom extractor." However, it is a small enough market that we have been able to hold our own as the iconic product. But we are always careful to say *pump* after the name. Protecting our brand is one of the reasons we developed the Sawyer Standard. Our "uncompromising commitment to quality and testing" isn't just a slogan; it's a promise we protect to the nth degree. Producing the best quality products in our markets will *always* set us apart from the competition. Good enough is not good enough at Sawyer.

> "Good enough" is not good enough.

Success will increase the need to protect your brand. Protecting your brand will also allow you to take advantage of brand equity, which, of course, feeds into trade equity. (All these things are connected.) So, if you release a product or service that disrupts the market—good for you! But remember the principle of unintended consequences. You will need to work harder to protect your brand after success.

Technology and Investment Barriers

Another way to protect your business is to focus on technology and investment barriers. Investment barriers include anything that makes it challenging for new investors to expand their business by entering your market. To put it very simply, if you make it costly for people to compete with you, then you're going to have fewer competitors. If investing in your market is expensive or complicated, or if it requires a specific expertise, location, or a significant investment in specialized technology, then fewer investors are going to risk competing with you.

The commercial airline industry is a great example. Good luck trying to start another airplane company! You've got Boeing, Airbus, Lockheed Martin, Gulfstream, and only a few other major manufacturers around the world.[40] If you were an investor interested in starting a new airplane manufacturing company, you would need to work through a series of tough questions: *How much technology goes into an airplane? What's the cost of building an airplane manufacturing plant? Can you hire or train a workforce to handle the complexity of the market you're entering?*

You're probably not going to invest unless you have a genuine passion for building airplanes and access to a lot of money. But if you're just looking for a solid return on your investment, there are other industries with fewer investment barriers than airplanes.

The takeaway here is that if your product is so complicated that others can't figure it out, or if your product requires so much money to build a new plant just to manufacture it—that's protection. That is the kind of protection Boeing has had for

---

40 There are other manufacturers who specialize in military-grade aircraft. In this discussion, we're focusing on commercial airplane manufacturing.

decades because few others have tried to make airplanes. And investment barriers don't always have to be about cost. Imagine again that you want to open a new restaurant. What if you could secure a corner location with good parking that no one else has access to? Isn't that a barrier to competing investors in the same town? So, technology and other investment barriers are a great way to protect your business. They keep the number of competitors low.

Determine the Present Value of New or Existing Customers

We're going to look at a simple example to illustrate this concept. For this example, it's helpful to assume that: (1) you, the investor, are looking for a minimum of a 10 percent return on your investment each year; and (2) your investment deteriorates by 10 percent every year due to profit expectation.

Now imagine that you sell your widget for ten dollars this year. You are going to make five dollars off of each sale, so each customer is worth five dollars in profit. Next year, you're going to sell them the same widget, but because a year has passed, each ten-dollar sale is only worth nine dollars in "today's dollars." You will make only $4.50 in profit on each of those sales.

In the third year, if you sell your customers the widget for ten dollars, it's now an $8.10 sale, making $4.05 of profit. In the next year, it's a $7.30 sale and $3.65 of profit, and so on. In terms of profit, you're still going to make your 10 percent ROI for a while, but you can see how the profit number drops each year by 10 percent in today's dollars. Here's a table that shows the decrease over five years.

Present Value Formula at 10 percent

	Sales Value ($)	Profit Value ($)	Total Present Value of Profit ($)
Year 1	10.00	5.00	5.00
Year 2	9.00	4.50	9.50
Year 3	8.10	4.05	13.55
Year 4	7.30	3.65	17.20
Year 5	6.60	3.29	20.49

This example assumes that your costs don't go up (which is a big assumption, but for the purposes of this exercise we won't think about increased costs yet. And price and cost should go up together, so we always default to "today's dollar.") The key takeaway is that each ten-dollar sale to your customers next year and each year after is worth less profit value than it is to you in year one.

So, in order to understand the value of your existing customers *today,* you need to look at each future sale in terms of *today's dollars*. As you work your way down in this example, you may discover that in today's dollars, though your sale for this year is ten dollars, that customer is actually worth $20.49 in today's dollars to you. That's what you're going to make if you sell to that customer for the next five years: $20.49 of today's dollars.

You might be asking why the dollars are worth less every year. Why is ten dollars this year only worth nine dollars next year? In economics terms, we're talking about the present value of future dollars. (Pull out your old college textbooks for a refresher.) The principal is that money received in the future is not worth as much as the same amount received today due to profit expectations.

As we've said, this simple example does not take increased costs into consideration. The costs for producing your widget will almost certainly go up, which decreases the amount of today's dollars you will make in the future. Though, at the same time, your price should increase in future years too due to recapturing inflation in your selling price. Thus, inflation in both the selling price and cost negates the need to factor inflation into this analysis.

But let's use Math Trap thinking again. Let's not factor in inflation or increased cost for the moment and return to our simple example. Why? Because you're probably not going to change your decisions whether those increases are there or not. If you can keep up with inflation, both on price and cost, then the spread between them stays the same as each year passes. What's important for making a decision for your business is that *today* you want a minimum 10 percent return on your investment, not just in producing the widget but in the marketing of it too. Factor in that your return decreases by 10 percent every year and that tells you what the customer is worth to you today and where you should cap your spending to get that customer.

But what if you did something to keep your costs low over multiple years? Say you purchased extra raw materials in year one, so your cost to make each widget was the same or less in year two and three. It's true. You could keep your ROI higher with this approach if you're early in the economies of scale.

If you are on the rapidly declining part of the curve (these could be either a manufacturing curve or a cost of advertising, PR, or social media curve) such that you are just cranking up the manufacturing or promotion of a new product and you are rapidly reducing your manufacturing and promotion cost, then you may want to factor that in. However, those benefits deteriorate rather quickly because of profit expectation. In that case, you can adjust the formula by adjusting the cost each year but still multiplying the year-two cost by 0.9, the year-three cost by 0.81, the year-four cost by 0.73, etc. Each year, the multiplier is reduced by multiplying it by 0.9 (in this example) or whatever your profit expectation is.

In our example, we used a 10 percent profit expectation to keep it simple. In the real world, you probably want to use a 20 percent profit expectation because, if you're considering an investment, you want to recoup your investment dollars. A 10 percent expectation beats the bank rates, but you may never get your original investment back in business. The 10 percent expectation may be good in the stock market because you generally get your investment dollars back when you sell. But, in manufacturing, the money is pretty much invested, the equipment wears out, the building gets old, and there is a deterioration of your initial investment.

Thus, Math Trap thinking "traps" the value of the lower manufacturing cost such that at a 20 percent run rate—unless you are really flying down the cost curve—it probably won't move your decision points much.[41]

Determining the value of your customers can grow in complexity. Not only can inflation rates and costs change, but you

---

[41] Keep in mind that I'm focused on small- to medium-sized businesses with these analyses. While there are nuggets in here for big and mature companies (like airplanes and autos, or a big idea in tech), some of these concepts will not be as relevant due to the sheer scale of their operations. And yet, when Jack Welch ran GE, he was a Math Trap-style thinker.

may also want to factor in different profit goals. Say you wanted a minimum of 20 percent profit rather than 10 percent, then obviously your return will deteriorate more quickly. The point is to protect and grow your business by thinking ahead. Think about the kind of future you want to engender for your business. Understanding the value of your existing customers will prevent you from overspending on customer acquisitions today and protect your business for the future.

Return to Your Life Cycle Curves

We've discussed the importance of understanding the life cycle curves at different points in this book. As you think about analyzing and protecting your business for future growth, then you need to pull it out once again. Ask yourself, where is my business on this curve? You've got to be able to answer this question honestly and with full understanding if you want to avoid the fates of other businesses. Because when that curve turns on you, you'll be in trouble. You'd better be ready.

This is true at Sawyer, of course. Certain products have a decreasing rate of increased sales. As we increase our household penetration, there are fewer new or first-time customers for these products and the curve transitions into repeat buyers. If the product has a long life, then this bends the curve quickly. But if you have a high repeat rate, such as a consumable or disposable product, the curve won't collapse as fast because you are less dependent on new customers. The life cycle curves for our products are something we think about and watch for regularly.

Being aware of where you are on the life cycle curves may help you make new products. For example, look at well-known brands like Oreos or Cheerios. You can buy many different types of each. Some flavors will stick and some will not. I guarantee the folks managing those brands are watching the life cycle curves on each new cookie and cereal product.

The alternative is to drive by looking in the rearview mirror. This is when you assume that you'll make the same amount next year as you did this year. But, of course, there's a point at which you run out of customers. (See the Weed Eater example in Chapter Four.) When you're on that side of the curve, you'll need to be careful to avoid overproducing and also strategic with your discounts. Doing so could save you lots of money depending on the size of your business.

Fundamentally understanding the life cycle curves is core. It's a part of "Sawyer think" and you should make it a part of your thinking too.

Listen to Your Customers (Again)

You should never stop listening to your customers. We've talked about the importance of doing so a few times in this book. But it's important to return to this idea again just briefly as you consider protecting your business's future.

As we've said, the easiest way to grow your business is to sell to existing customers. This works on both the consumer and the trade level (your retailers). If you're a toothpaste company, you can probably get the average person who uses your toothpaste to also try your new mouthwash. This is the consumer level. If you're a high-performance outdoor company like Sawyer, then you can probably work with your retail partners to secure one more line item on their PO for a new kind of filter or insect repellent. This is the trade level.

The bottom line is that you can't ever stop listening. Even if your business is mature, don't make the mistake of thinking that you fully understand your customers today. Customers will change (that's Creative Destruction). Just look at the younger generations and how quickly they change what they want. Keep up the focus groups, the shopper intercepts, the phone and text campaigns, and social media surveys. There are 3.6 million babies born in the United States each year. That also means about 3.6 million new customers are aging into your market each year too. What have you heard from them? What generation or people group is entering or exiting your market? They are all different. At Sawyer, we spend a great deal of effort understanding the different generations—how they think, what they like to do, and how we should communicate differently with them from other generations. We are constantly changing or segmenting our communications and products to adapt to our incoming customers.

Why We Protect Our Business: A Daily Necessity

Here is another one of Darrel Larson's stories from his travels as Sawyer's International Director:

> "A Liberian man took me to his water source," Darrel told me. "It was rust-colored and nasty. Then he bent down and started lapping it up." As the man sat on his knees by the water's edge, he told Darrel, "This is the water we drink every day." After he finished, he pulled out anti-diarrhea meds. "I carry these everywhere," he said.

Darrel learned that this man and many others in his village carry diarrhea meds with them every day, everywhere they go. It's a daily necessity because the water they drink is so contaminated. Anti-diarrhea meds are just part of the normal routine of their days. It's heartbreaking. What's worse is that most people who live in the bush can't even afford to have that kind of medicine.

In this chapter, we've discussed how you can protect your business. If all goes well, your business will grow. As our water filter business grew, it made sense for us to become more and more involved in clean water initiatives around the world, initiatives that may someday create a future in which people like this Liberian man no longer have to take anti-diarrhea medicine the way we take daily vitamin supplements.

What future is your business working toward? If your business grows as you hope it will, what will you do with its profits?

Chapter Ten

Packaging and More

The human mind processes many thousands of pieces of information every day. *Fast Company* reported that by 2011, Americans were taking in five times as much information as they did in 1986.[42] With our smartphones, tablets, and other devices, you can imagine how much that number has increased since then! It's up to you to compete with all of that information to get your message across and sell your product or service. It's a chaotic contest between myriad information and short attention spans.

In this chapter, we will discuss techniques for communicating with your target customers effectively and quickly. We will begin by discussing packaging strategies Sawyer uses for our products. But these strategies can apply beyond our channels of distribu-

---

42   Daniel J. Levitin, "Why It's So Hard To Pay Attention, Explained By Science," *Fast Company,* September 23, 2015, https://www.fastcompany.com/3051417/why-its-so-hard-to-pay-attention-explained-by-science.

tion. They can also apply to other communications such as posters, displays, flyers, mailers, etc. We will address those at the end.

A good rule of thumb is to assume that you have *less than two seconds* to grab a person's attention and begin the process of convincing them to buy your product. In those two seconds, you have to do at least four things.

Four Principles for Effective Packaging

One: *Tell them who you are.* Whether you are well-established or just starting, you need to introduce your brand or relay its power. As we discussed in Chapter Nine, investing in brand equity is one way to protect your business. Your brand should be prominent in everything you do.

Two: *Make the product name obvious.* Do you have products with different names than your brand? Sawyer has products like the Squeeze Filter and Mini Filter. These names obviously have to be noticeable on the packaging as well. Whatever the name of your product is, it must be easily noticeable. It sets up your product line.

In the case of big-name brands such as Wheat Thins, the product name is typically more prominent than the corporate (brand) name Nabisco. Manufacturers of products with strong brand equity like this (again, see Chapter Nine) will have to figure out which name gets the most prominence. How you deal with the ranking of importance between the brand name and the product name depends on where you are in the life cycle curve of the product and brand.

Three: *Tell the customer what you are selling.* Your product will face a lot of "clutter" in a retail store. Just look at the camping department shelves. Our products are not only competing with other insect repellents, but we're also up against big-ticket items like tents, sleeping bags, coolers, and a wide variety of camping accessories that fill a consumer's field of vision. It's imperative that your packaging cuts through all of this visual clutter.

What if you've earned the privilege of being selected for the checkout counters? Now you are up against an extensive variety of products—candy, soft drinks, lip balm, sunglasses, and numerous other items. In Sawyer's case, we may be the only insect repellent there, so we must make sure that the person checking out knows what our products are. Consumers standing in the checkout line might not have gone to the store looking for something from Sawyer's product category, so we try to create "impulse" sales. You should too.

When your product is sold in a section dedicated to your product category, it can be a little easier. If you're well known enough, such as OFF!® or Coppertone, having to proclaim that the product is an insect repellent or sunscreen is not as important, and you can put more focus on the final principle for effective packaging.

Four: *Make your product stand out*. If the shelves around your product are filled with mostly dark colors, go with a lighter color or white. If light-colored packaging dominates the area, go with a dark color.

Take Every Square Inch

It goes without saying that you should take all the square and cubic footage the retailer will give you. When we are given seven inches of width to work with, we shoot for a package that is 6.875 inches wide. This leaves 1/16 of an inch clearance on each side so that it doesn't rub the next product over. If two of our products are next to each other, that totals 1/8 of an inch clearance combined. The same is true for the height and depth. Many competitors leave big gaps. They may stop at 6.5 inches wide. That is a waste of "billboard" advertising and leaves "air" gaps in the planogram, which irritates consumers' eyes.

We also take great pains to make sure our units are balanced. This is not as easy as you think with water filters. We are meticulous in design and production with balance. A cockeyed unit on the shelf looks horrible and unappealing to the consumer. It can also mess up the product next to it (especially if it is another one of our products).

The point is, whether you're using cardboard or plastic clamshells, take every bit of space they'll give you. All of it is valuable "billboard" space you can use to sell your product to the consumer. By leaving just 1/16 of an inch clearance around the sides of your packaging, you'll have a clean, appealing presentation of your product.

The Secret Sauce

In addition to taking all the space the retailer will give us, as well as the core principles we just covered, Sawyer uses four other tactics for getting the most out of our packaging. I think of these tactics as the secret sauce of excellent product packaging.

One: *Add a shiny object*. A *shiny object* is a design element—a band of distinct color, a sunburst, etc.—that steals the consumer's attention from the other products. Our shiny object on the water filters is a red bar across the bottom of each package. To the extent that we can, the red bars will also be in a straight line across packages of similar size. When the consumer looks at a shelf of Sawyer products, they should see a long red bar stretching from package to package, gaining even more attention. We also put the brand name and the product names in the same spot on each package for added impact and clarity.

Sawyer uses small print within our shiny object (the red bar). We only want to grab the consumer's attention while they are still in the aisle and not overshadow our other more important points. Think through which color you will use carefully. Red, blue, and yellow are strong options because they're primary colors. So is white. Most importantly, choose the color that best contrasts with the rest of the package.

You can also achieve the effect of a shiny object through *violators*. A violator is a word or a point of emphasis placed at a slight diagonal. In the United States, we are used to reading left to right, top to bottom. When you put something at a slight angle, the mind wants to deal with that right away because it violates the normal order for reading.

A violator is a big card to play as it can sometimes cover your other points of emphasis, so play it well. It may be the first thing the customer reads. Speaking of violators . . .

Two: *Violate the aisle.* The second ingredient in our secret sauce is to have our product packaging violate the aisle. We know the depth of each retailer's pegs or shelves. Some are twelve inches, some fourteen inches, and some are six inches. Some retailers use slat boards instead of pegs. Slat shelves can significantly influence the height of your product more than pegs would. Slat shelving also uses pegs, which will determine your depth.

No matter what the retailer uses, we try to make the depth of our packaging just deep enough so that when the peg is full the unit on the end of the peg sticks out an inch or more into the aisle. This extra inch adds to our visibility and reduces the visual competition of the products next to us.

One time, this created a problem when we designed clamshell packaging for a major retailer that used fourteen-inch pegs. Another retailer who used six-inch pegs on their endcaps could not put the same clamshells on their endcaps because they could only go one unit deep. Because the product sold out over the weekends while they were too busy to replenish the endcap, they lost sales on some very important real estate and thus picked other products for the endcap instead of our filters. We redesigned the clamshells to be a little wider and less deep so that they could put two units on a peg for the endcap displays. The endcaps emptied much less often on the weekends, and everyone enjoyed more sales. Twelve years later, we are still on the endcaps.

Three: *Carefully consider the sequence of how a consumer examines your product to determine the importance of each side of the packaging.* Obviously, the front is the most important side of every package. So, at Sawyer, we do all the things we've already discussed. But once a consumer picks up a product and looks at the front of a package, what is the most likely side they will turn to next?

Since 87 percent of the population is right-handed, it used to be true that most people would pick up a unit with their left hand. (Think of how baseball and softball gloves are on the left hand for righties. The left hand does the catching.) Then they would comfortably turn the product so the right-hand side of the package became visible. (Think of turning a doorknob counterclockwise with your left hand. It's a very comfortable, common motion for right-handed people.) The back of the packaging would then be the third visible side, and the left side of the packaging would be the last.

This pattern doesn't work anymore. Now, every consumer carries a cell phone. Some people carry their cell phone in their dominant hand, while others carry their phone in their non-dominant hand. As a result, we consider both the right side and the left side of the package as potentially being side two. We have adjusted our messaging accordingly. Both sides are pretty similar now. The front engages the customer while the back closes the deal. (More on that later.)

Some of our repellents are heavy, so they end up on the bottom shelf. Even the ones that are not heavy could end up on the lower pegs, so we have to rely on the top of the packaging to make important marketing messages visible. In situations like these, we use a *cathedral header*. Instead of being a flat top on a package, a cathedral header is a forty-five-degree angle on top. It adds an inch or two to the height of the package, so be careful to stay within the vertical space of the retailer's shelves or pegs if they use slats. The cathedral top also adds cost to the product, but as we say at Sawyer, "The most expensive product is the one that doesn't sell." In other words, it's better to spend the extra cents required on the packaging to make your product sell than to have it gathering dust in inventory.

> **"The most expensive product is the one that doesn't sell."**

Four: *Understand the difference between features and benefits.* Remember the classic marketing principle: you sell features, but the consumer buys benefits. The consumer wants a peaceful day outdoors without the nuisance of bug bites; we sell them repellents. The consumer wants peace of mind about the water they drink while they're hiking; we sell them a filter. The consumer wants to lose weight; someone sells them a cookbook of low-fat recipes. Therefore, list your top-selling benefits on your packaging. If you have room, you may choose to razzle-dazzle the customer with some techy feature, so long as it ends in proclaiming a benefit for the consumer.

Unfortunately, depending on the size of the package, you only get to put one or at most two key features or benefits on the front. Leave "air" or visual space on the front so that people can absorb the brand, the product name, the product category, the shiny object, and the key benefit or benefits. Avoid throwing all your stuff here. Leave the front visually pleasing. If appropriate, put a feature benefit into the shiny object. Established products will often use "NEW" or "Improved" as their violator.

We place the "Sawyer Standard" in small print inside the violator. We let the red bar do its primary job of attracting the eye from four or more feet away. Then the consumer will read the Sawyer Standard (which builds brand equity) once they're closer to the product. Some companies place a key benefit in the violator: "Fat-Free," "Improved formula," etc. Sawyer chooses not to.

Once the front is designed, you can repeat or add more feature benefits to both sides. The back panel is your deal closer. Let loose your feature benefits as if you were making a personal presentation. However, you must walk the customer logically through the argument and in a manner in which they think and absorb information, not according to your thought process. Do this by having non-invested people review the process. Remember to leave some "air" on the back panel as well. The font, pictures, and diagrams must be large enough to read easily. If you need space to explain more, then say something like, "Directions are included" or "Visit brand.com/tellmemore."

Putting this all together, we have a sequence of questions we like to ask to see if our packaging works as well as it can.

1. Does the customer pick up on our shiny object or other distinctive qualities when they turn the corner on the aisle?
2. At two or three feet away, do they know what we are selling?
3. When they stand in front of our product, do they know the product category, our best points of difference or our best benefits versus other brands in this category, our brand, and the product name—in that sequence? If so, that is a successful front panel.
4. As they turn the product to the left or right, do they understand some of our other benefits?
5. When they read the back, did we close the deal?

Questions 1 and 2 need to happen in less than two seconds. For question 3, you have a few more seconds. With questions 4 and 5, you have as long as the customer wishes to engage.

If they pick it up, we believe you have about a 70 percent chance of making the sale. If they read the back, your odds improve to 90 percent.

An example of "the Mini" in its packaging.

As I mentioned earlier, many of these same concepts apply to posters, displays, flyers, mailers, etc. Pick distinctive but not hard-to-read colors. Keep your key points simple and easy to read and absorb. If you have a longer message that needs to be conveyed (not just a message you *want* to convey), then use the back of the page, inside the flyer, or significantly drop the font size on the front. If you hook them, they will read the small stuff.

This is Sawyer's secret sauce for packaging. This is how we cut through the noise of the thousands of pieces of information that consumers' brains are bombarded with every day. All of these principles may not apply to what you are doing, but some surely will.

The Marshall Islands Project

One of the most beautiful places on earth is also one of the least visited. The Marshall Islands are a string of small volcanic islands, islets, and atolls (an island made of a ring of coral around a lagoon) in the South Pacific. Imagine Australia on a map, then go up and to the right. Among the thousands of islands that litter that part of the ocean are the Marshall Islands, home to tropical beaches, beautiful coral reefs, and water that is rich with hues of blue, turquoise, and aquamarine. A drone shot of the islands looks like the setting of a movie or a cover spread for *National Geographic*. They're amazing.

But the Marshall Islands are hard to reach. Their people are poor, and there is no significant infrastructure for tourism. And, of course, the drinking water is bad, even life-threatening. The people of the Marshall Islands have long depended upon rainwater as their primary water source. Like many countries that rely on rainwater, their water is filled with E. coli from bird feces covering the metal roofs of their houses, which is then washed into their supply.

But in July 2023, the Marshall Islands became the second developing nation in the world to receive border-to-border access to clean water according to the UN Sustainability Goal #6.[43] This monumental effort was led by a small, local, women-led group called Kora in Okrane (KIO). Over a five-year period, Sawyer partnered with the women of KIO to ensure that every household in the Marshall Islands—representing more than 42,000 lives spread across more than 1,150 islands and islets—had access to clean drinking water. The Sawyer International Bucket System and the Sawyer Tap Water Filtration System were the primary means for providing this access. They're both easy to operate and maintain. With proper care, every filter lasts ten years or more and removes 99.99999 percent of all bacteria, 99.9999 percent of all protozoa, and 100 percent of microplastics. Our GIS tracking shows that cases of diarrhea have been reduced by more than 90 percent since the filters were installed.

This project comprised the best of Sawyer's clean water efforts: indigenous leadership with a big vision, easy and affordable clean water systems, dedicated local teams, and cutting-edge technology to implement the project and track its success. However, something else made the Marshall Islands project unique. The very first recipient was Nalia, a young girl on one of the most remote islands, an atoll called Arno. Most projects like this start in the center of a given country—the biggest city, the capi-

---

43   https://sdgs.un.org/goals/goal6. The first developing nation to reach this milestone was Liberia in 2020.

tal, or the largest island. But in this instance, KIO chose to start on the outer rim and work their way in. Their rationale? "Those people are the most vulnerable and have the greatest needs."

The project began in Arno in 2018. After a brief stoppage due to the coronavirus pandemic, the project resumed and eventually finished on the main island, Majuro. A few Sawyer staff members were there for the celebration on the day they finished. Today, KIO and Sawyer are working together to provide access to clean water to every classroom in every school in the Marshall Islands, as well as every medical clinic.

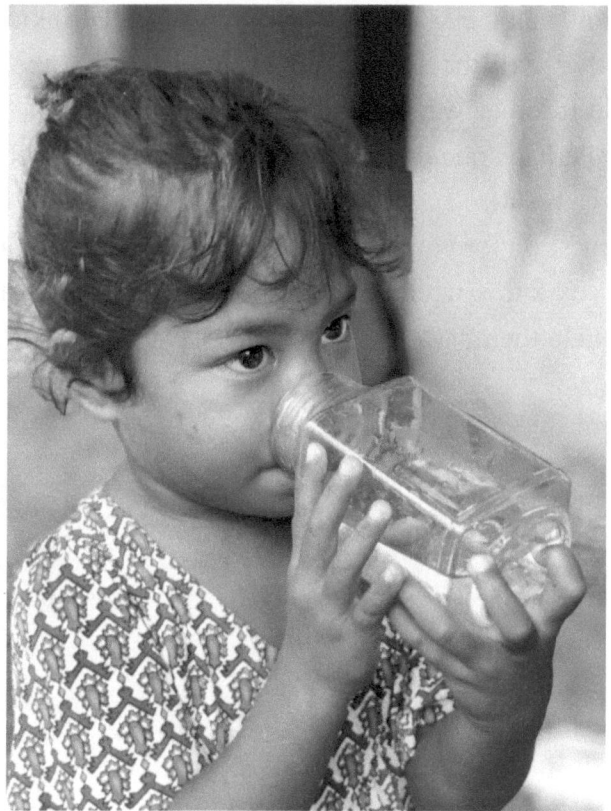

This is Nalia on Arno, taking her first sip of clean drinking water.

Like every other story in this book, I take no personal credit for any of this. Dedicated local leaders with a big vision and the amazing staff at Sawyer are the ones who make stories like this happen. I'm a marketing guy, and I like being one. In this chapter, I've shared the secret sauce of packaging products that was developed over decades of work with retailers. It's a recipe that has made Sawyer products stand out no matter where they're being sold. This approach to packaging has also helped put Sawyer in the position to help people who have big visions, like the one it took to complete the Marshall Islands project. Who knows, now that the Marshall Islands have clean drinking water, perhaps there will be a ripple effect that improves the lives of its people in other ways. (Our research indicates that this *will* happen.) Perhaps one day more people will visit these beautiful islands as a result.

My question for you is: What will you do with your success? Who do you know with a big, world-changing vision, and how will you help them?

Chapter Eleven
Incremental Variable Cost

Although we started the company in 1984, Sawyer didn't make any money until 2009 (other than the Gulf War years).[44] That means for about twenty-three of our first twenty-five years we didn't make any profit. We had many lean years. How come the business didn't close? And how did we start making the money we make today, which allows us to give so much away?

The answer to these questions has to do with a few principles we'll discuss in this chapter. But before we get to those answers, you need to ask yourself an important question about your business: What type of business do you have?

Three Types of Businesses

There are three types of businesses: growing, flat, and declining.

---

44 During Operation Desert Shield, we produced sunblock for the US military. During Operation Desert Storm, we produced the military's insect repellent.

Types of Businesses

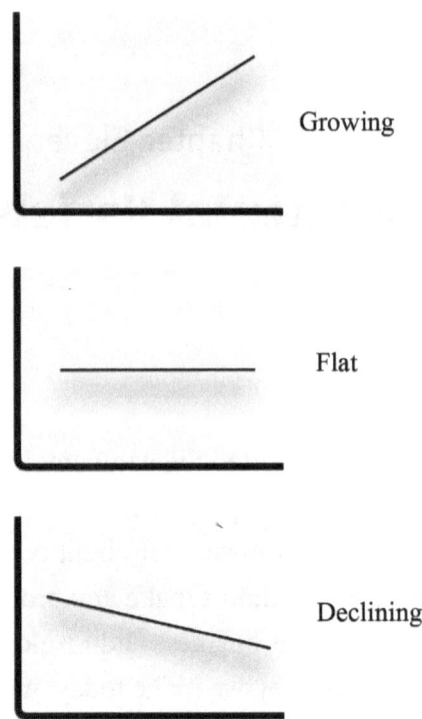

Your strategy will change depending on which type best describes your business. We're going to discuss some core economic principles that apply to all three. Sawyer has been growing for thirty-four years, so I will start by discussing these principles in the context of a growing business.

Here are some quick questions to determine which type best describes your business:

1. What has been your five- or ten-year sales trend?
2. What is the honest assessment of where your sales should go from here? No rose-colored glasses. No hockey stick

forecasts, where a flat or downward trending line suddenly shoots upward, looking like the blade of a hockey stick.
3. Is there anything that will change in your business that could change that trajectory? Creative Destruction in your market? Or internal changes such as a change in ownership or management? (Think about what is in front of you that wasn't there in the past.)

Some words of caution: most people think their business is always growing, even when that isn't the case. This can be dangerous. If your business is actually declining and you don't pay attention to the core economic principles we'll discuss, you can get clobbered.

Several years of a 2 percent or more decline should throw up a red flag. If the trend continues, and if you do not change your overhead structure, then you will put yourself out of business. Slow declines like this will test your emotions. *When do you let longtime employees go? When do you stop Christmas bonuses?* These are hard decisions. Big corporations usually turn such divisions into "cash cows." They stop investments, then cut overhead to the minimum or consolidate overhead into another division, and finally ride the sales down until no profits remain. Entrepreneurs in this situation may want to sell their business and cash out—often to a company or person who can do what a big corporation would do, i.e., "cash cow" it out.

And if you're banking on a hockey stick strategy (reversing declines into growth), be honest with yourself. Is there a real reason to justify that? In my experience, most hockey stick strategies are optimistic, wishful thinking. They don't recognize reality. The passions of the management or the owners are getting in the way of a true assessment. "Maybe the new road will finally be completed." Or "maybe people will reacquire the taste for licorice." Or "maybe a new movie will feature our widget and make it a hot item." These things can happen, but more often the decline continues anyway. That said, you can manage the decline down profitably if you recognize reality and make the hard decisions.

Now that you know which type best describes your business, the first two principles to pay attention to are (1) set prices for where you're going to be, not to where you are. The second is more abstract: (2) get the money going through your hands, and then learn how to keep it.

In order to accurately set prices for where you're going to be, you need to understand your Direct Cost Curve.

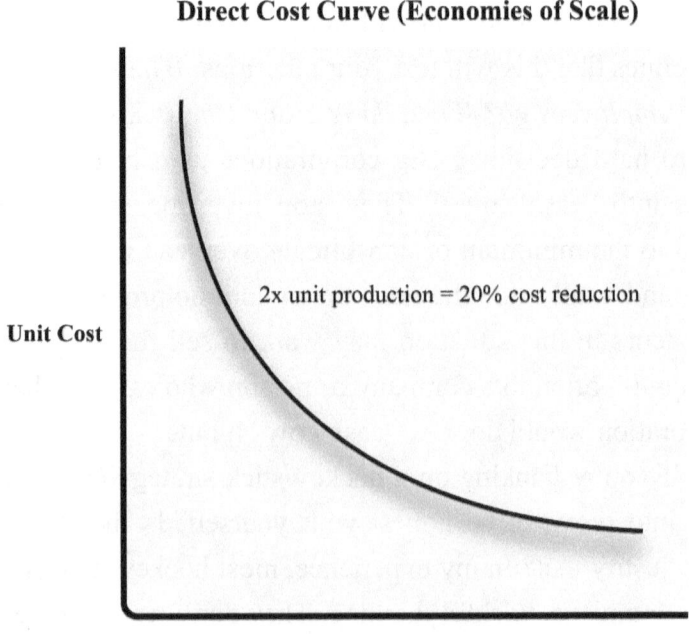

Direct Cost Curve (Economies of Scale)

2x unit production = 20% cost reduction

Unit Cost

Cumulative Production

The Direct Cost Curve reveals an important economic idea: *every time you double your production, you reduce your cost by 20 percent*. This is usually called the economies of scale.

As an example, imagine that you invented the first washing machine. Your cost to produce a few machines was incredibly high when you first started, but as they quickly gained popularity, your production doubled, doubled again, and then doubled again. With each doubling your cost dropped. Ten or twenty years later and there are countless washing machines on the market. Now it becomes a real challenge for anyone working at your company to reduce the cost of one of your washing machines. Because so many of them have already been made, you're very unlikely to double the production number again. This is the Direct Cost Curve in action.

The slope of a Direct Cost Curve is great in the beginning. You're way up on the curve, making your first widgets, and each time you double production you really come down in cost. What entrepreneur doesn't love that? But like the washing machine example, once your product has been out in the market for a while it becomes more difficult to reduce costs. This is why growing businesses can price products for *where they will be down the curve*, when their costs are low, and not where they are at the beginning of the curve. With the lower price you'll get more sales and get to your lower cost sooner.

The next commonly misunderstood principle regards how to get money going through your hands and then learning how to keep it. The first thing a growing business needs to do is focus on sales and getting money to come in. It may seem simple, but I've seen many entrepreneurs and others who work for growing businesses forget this key principle. It's not until *after* you get money going through your hands that you can really learn how to profit from it.

These two principles are pure economics. They're from the Macroeconomics 101 course you took in college, but so many of us forget them from time to time. They are also the foundation for the lesser-known principle we'll discuss, Incremental Variable Cost.

What Does It Cost Me to Make One More Widget?

This is a great question for any entrepreneur or business to ask. You need to ask it because future thinking is what will lead you to greater profits.

More specifically, ask yourself, "Right now, if I were to sell one more widget, what would my incremental variable cost be?" This is an important question that a lot of people can't get past.

This is also a question that accountants shouldn't help you with. Accountants tend to get in the way when you try to answer this question. Don't let them. Accountants can mess you up big time. When determining costs, accountants will want you to include the overhead you're absorbing, but that isn't necessary to focus on right now. You just need to know, if I make one more widget, how much will it cost?

In order to answer this question, you first need to consider your *direct cost*. Any business or economics book will tell you that direct costs are your expenses for making a product or delivering a service. This includes:

- Raw materials
    - the cost of the inbound freight
    - the cost of inventory

- Direct labor
  - average wage
  - taxes
  - insurance (including workers' comp, etc.)

We're going to take a closer look at a few of these. Let's start with the cost of inventory.

Typically, there are three methods for determining the cost of your inventory: LIFO, FIFO, and average.

LIFO stands for last in, first out. Think of it this way: You bought something a year ago for one dollar. Then you bought the same thing today, but it cost you $1.25. The LIFO method says the next one out of the door will cost you $1.25.

FIFO stands for first in, first out. So, if you bought something for one dollar a year ago and now it's $1.25, you will still measure the sale as costing you one dollar until you burn off all of the old inventory.

The third method for determining the cost of your inventory is average. (This is sometimes called the weighted-average method.) Average is just how it sounds: you assign a cost to your inventory based on the total cost of goods purchased or produced (within a certain period) divided by the total number of items purchased or produced. It moves toward the LIFO number as you use up the order inventory.

Depending on the size of your inventory, interest rates, and other factors, LIFO, FIFO, and average all have advantages or disadvantages. It's best to let the accountants run the business the way they want to run the business (that you've agreed to), but from an analytical point of view, you need to ask, "If I'm going to make one more widget, what am I going to pay for those raw materials?" So, regardless of what you paid before, you always want to think about LIFO. This is future thinking—where you're going, not where you are.

Direct labor is the cost for your workers to assemble your product: gross pay, plus matching deduction, plus variable insurance. This means your analysis includes not only what you pay them but also what you have to deduct, such as the matching portion of Social Security, Medicare and Medicaid, worker's comp, health insurance, etc. All those things are tied directly to the dollar-per-hour labor.

Once you have all these numbers, you can determine the Direct Cost to make one more widget tomorrow.

Indirect Cost

Indirect costs include:

- Supervisors
- Non-line workers (custodial, etc.)
- Equipment
- Manufacturing facilities
- Outbound shipping

Indirect costs don't go away. But they also don't increase when one more widget is made. Instead, they increase in chunks.

For example, if you have a supervisor who oversees the work of ten people and you give her one more person, the cost of that supervisor doesn't necessarily increase. She might have the capacity to supervise twelve people.

All of these things go up in segments. Supervisors increase when you hire a new supervisor. Non-line workers (like janitors, etc.) only increase if you need to hire more.

Fully Absorbed Cost

The next cost to consider is your Fully Absorbed Cost. This is where your accounts should come in. It includes your overhead office staff, sales staff, advertising, PR, insurance, rent—all of your expenses not directly connected to making your product. That is, everything you have to pay for to stay in business.

But where it gets dangerous is if you try to apply overhead to this incremental growth business because you can probably make one more widget without changing any of these costs. You can come back and analyze your Fully Absorbed Costs in more detail later. But right now, you want to know your incremental cost to make one more widget, from which you'll set your incremental price, which will lead you to incremental profit. So, for this exercise, let's hold overhead steady and ignore it until later.

Total Cost Curve

Let's say you figured it cost you ten dollars to make your widget. And when you sell it, you sell it for twenty dollars. You make ten dollars. You use that ten dollars to cover all your fixed costs, represented by the area under the cost line on the chart. The total for these fixed costs isn't going to move. You can sell one more at twenty dollars. It cost ten dollars to make one more. But your fixed cost doesn't change, so the total ten dollars made from the save drops completely to the profit line.

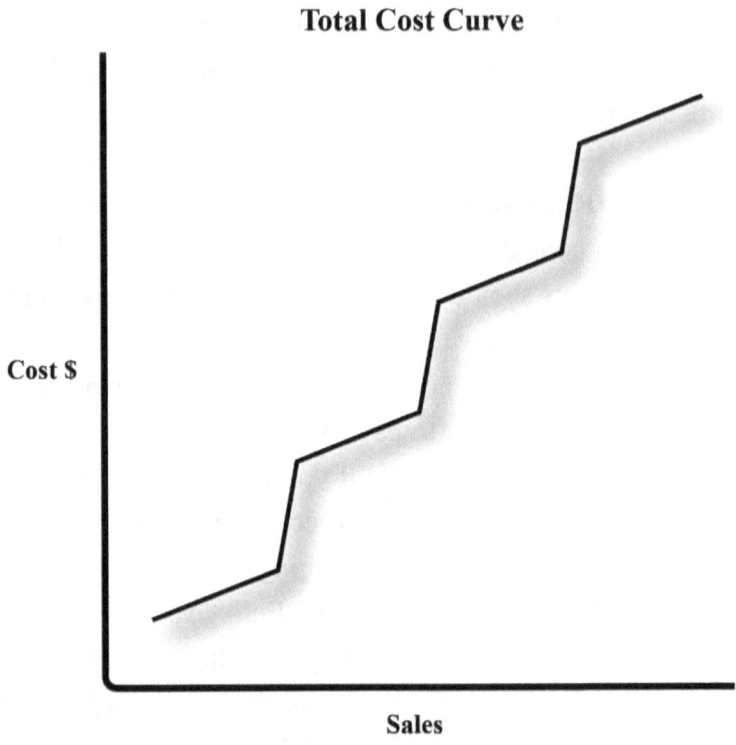

Total Cost Curve

The almost parallel lines (to the sales line) represent your incremental costs of making one more widget. Now those costs move along until you have to increase one of your fixed costs. For instance, you may need to buy a new forklift for the warehouse, get a new building, or add another supervisor.

So, this chart shows these little bands where you can you can sell something without having to increase any of the fixed costs. It's just pure incremental variable profit. Once in a while, your cost has got to jump up because you need to put a fixed cost in. Plus, making one more widget or ten thousand more widgets helps you go down the economies of scale curve more quickly.

Determining Your Price

Here's the thing to remember: these ideas are all based on increasing sales, so the actual cost per unit is going down. When your business is growing, ask yourself, "Where can I get our costs to be?"

We know that if we sell a million units of one of our products, we're going to have a certain cost. But if we double it to two million, we know it's going to cost us 20 percent less. So, we price our product to where we're going to be, not where we are. At the end of the day, you spend dollars, not percents.

> **At the end of the day, you spend dollars, not percents.**

I started this chapter by telling you how Sawyer was *not* making money during most of our early years. One of the reasons for that was the cost of travel. I didn't understand guerrilla marketing until after a few years of spending way too much money on conventional advertising. This was a costly mistake. But then, even after I realized that we needed to travel from store to store building relationships and telling the world about our products, there were still high travel costs.

Another reason we weren't profitable for many years was that we kept investing in technology. During most of those years, we could have made a profit if we had throttled back, but we didn't want to. We chose to invest in tooling, packaging, and everything else needed to charge forward. Doing so was future thinking. It would set us up for where we wanted to be. Though we were losing money from the accountant's point of view, the bank was happy because we had the ability to make profits.

But then we released a product that just exploded.

The Sawyer Mini

In 2005, we released our first .1 micron absolute water filter. This was in large part due to the engineering genius of Sawyer's lead engineer, John Smith. He helped us develop what would become the Sawyer Standard: .1 micron absolute and testing three different times during manufacturing. By 2006 the Sawyer Squeeze was moving along on the retail side of the business. We offered two versions: a full gravity system for $89.99 and just the "Squeeze" filter with a pouch for $39.99. The technology of a .1 micron absolute filter was (and is) unmatched in the marketplace. Word started to spread among the early educators and early innovators that make up our place on the bell curve. The Squeeze ultimately changed the way people use filters in the field, and we eventually discontinued the gravity system.

However, from 2005 through 2006, we received feedback stating that consumers wanted the Squeeze to weigh less. The total weight was only three and a half ounces, but every ounce matters to serious hikers and outdoorsmen. They continued to ask, "Could you reduce the weight?"

Thanks again to John's genius, we were able to cut the diameter of the water filter in half while keeping its length. This new filter had half as many fibers, but it was still .1 micron absolute *and* it only weighed 1.4 ounces—less than half of the Squeeze. It also still lasted for up to one hundred thousand gallons. So, in 2007, the Sawyer Mini Water Filtration System was born.

But the success of the "Mini" wasn't just due to the technology or the weight. We also used the first principle outlined above and priced it to where we wanted to be, not where we were at the time. It was essential for us to keep it under twenty dollars. Every marketer knows that $19.97 and $19.99 are magic price points.[45] Though the Mini wasn't that much cheaper to make than the Sawyer Squeeze, we released it at $19.99, knowing that if we could double our production, we'd reduce our cost by 20 percent, making our price to the consumers much more viable.

The Mini was a major disruption in the water filter market. It became our number one selling model and still is to this day. To put this into context, the entire water filter market for hikers in 2001 was about eighty thousand units per year (ceramic, fiber matrix, and other types), with an average cost of around eighty-nine dollars each. Today, the market is well over a million units per year, with our number one selling filter still priced very low. That is called market disruption.

The principles of Incremental Variable Cost were in play, and we were able to reduce our cost and increase the money going through our hands. Then we had another disruptive, world-changing experience connected to the Mini: we met the folks at Compassion International.

We first met Compassion International—an organization dedicated to freeing children from poverty—at an Accord Christian conference in 2009. We soon began sending filters to their sponsored children around the globe. When the 2010 earthquake devastated Haiti, Compassion asked us to send *seventy-five thousand filter systems* to the kids they sponsored there. We then partnered with another charity dedicated to providing access to clean water called Waves for Water. They had

---

45 These price points are less "magical" today as we move to a cashless society.

a partner in Haiti named Magepa, which was able to import the filters through the chaos, source the buckets we needed, and distribute the filters quickly.[46]

The Compassion distribution of our filters in Haiti put us on the map in a new way when it comes to clean water. It was a major disruption of the market at the time. Not only was this project sizable, but it was also highly visible and gave Sawyer its first big credibility that our filters worked as promised: life-saving, life-changing.

How Managing Overhead Can Help You Manage Costs

For most of this chapter, we've been considering these ideas from the perspective of a growing business. However, you may be in a declining business now or in the future. So, what should be considered?

When you're in decline, you must manage your cost far more than managing your price. If you truly understand your business, then you should be able to identify variable costs, semi-variable costs, and fixed costs. When in decline, you've got to get rid of more and more of the fixed and semi-fixed costs. That's when it's time to sell one of your two forklifts. You don't need it. Or it's time to get out of one of the buildings. You don't need it. Or unfortunately, it's time to lay off the salesforce. You only need two instead of four. Fixed costs will back up on you quickly when you're in decline if you don't understand incremental, semi-fixed, and fixed costs, both in the direct cost and then the overhead cost. It will come to get you real fast.

---

46 We still work with Waves for Water and Magepa to this day. Sawyer has partnerships with more than twenty NGOs working in Haiti today.

If you understand all these things, then a sensitivity analysis becomes very easy. If you have good high margins and growth opportunities, then you focus on growing your sales while holding your overhead. If your margins are low, or you're on the decline, you need to focus on cutting your direct, semi-variable, and overhead costs.

With high margins, you want to grow like crazy, and you spend to grow while managing the overhead.

With low margins, you focus on cutting costs and managing your overhead, especially when you're in decline. You must watch the overhead when you're on the way down. Someone might say, "I can't let Johnny go. He's been with us for twenty-five years." I know it's uncomfortable, but you know what? If you don't let Johnny go, then you may all go.

I once heard a seasoned CEO say that you should eliminate 10 percent of your workforce who do not have direct contact with your customers each year. You can instead outsource those specific tasks. Now, I don't follow this CEO's advice to the extreme. But it certainly sets a mindset that says, "Why do anything that you don't really need to do?" For example, at Sawyer we outsource every piece of manufacturing that becomes repetitive and that we don't want or need to do ourselves. There are people who love to manufacture goods and that's great. We outsource some of our manufacturing to them and count them as great partners. We also outsource IT because we don't need an internal IT person at this point. Why spend the money required to hire one?

But some people like to gather all the hens. They want to manage everything. But it's helpful to ask, do you really need to have in-house accountants? Similarly, do you really need to hire somebody to clean the restrooms and mop the floor? Or, can you work with a local business that will bring custodians in? Do you really need to hire IT people, or can you work with a provider that will give you access to a team of people when you need them? Nothing says it's wrong to hire an outside custodial service or an IT provider instead of hiring a janitor or IT manager on your staff. It's still their job. They are still making money. You're just paying the service provider and you're not having to manage the people. You're taking less risk, doing less paperwork, and putting more focus on what generates profits for you.

Nothing is wrong with working with outside accountants either. What if you had three accountants on staff? Then, one day you realize you need three *and a half* accountants. How do you add half a person inside the company? You can't. But it's easy if you outsource your accounting. Your service provider will have part of an accountant's time assigned to your account. You couldn't make the same jump in-house. You'd have to bite the bullet and hire a fourth person to fill half a role's work. Then they're not fully utilized, but you're still paying the full cost for that person. It is these jumps in fixed and semi-fixed costs that you need to evaluate carefully. Do you really need to buy that forklift? Or can you rent that forklift? This advice is especially useful for small or declining businesses.

Jack Welch used to ask, "Why do you do R & D in-house?" Why not have some R & D people but also get your ideas from outside? Do you need to put all that infrastructure in place to do the research in-house? Cutting-edge research can come from many places. R & D in-house is meant to review the ideas from outside and generate new ideas.

I jokingly tell people, "I'd like to be God if it weren't for the people." What I mean is that it's not in Sawyer's best interest to manage more people when we can outsource certain tasks. We'd rather let other people manage them so we can focus on developing better products and more sales. Outsourcing is not a bad thing.

The big question behind all of these questions is: Does is it really help you sell your product and manage your costs by hiring someone on staff for that specific role? This is a new way of thinking for some people, but it's worth asking these questions, especially if your business is declining.

Think about the things that make you money and that are key to your success. Those are the things to focus on. (Or, what *will be* the key to your success, if you're just starting.) From our perspective, manufacturing is a low-margin business while innovation and technology are high-margin businesses. In practical terms, this means that Sawyer has a social media team on staff. We keep people in that role so we can make changes to our online accounts quickly (innovation and technology). It's key to our success. At the same time, we outsource the low-margin parts of the business (manufacturing) every chance we can.

So, which tasks are key to your success? What makes you money?

Managing your costs is in your margins. Are you high margin or low margin? You never want to ignore your overhead. You've always got to manage overhead, regardless of your margins. But if you're low margin, it can mean life or death.

Conclusion

None of this would've happened for Sawyer Products if we hadn't spent many years investing in the tooling and technology that made us a disruptor in the water filter market. Future thinking pays dividends.

It also wouldn't have happened if we didn't listen to our consumers. We already discussed the importance of listening. In those early years, I visited sixty to eighty retail stores each year. I and others would sit there for twelve hours and talk to everyone about the Extractor™ Pump Kit, repellents, and water filters. We got good at listening. Now, it's social media influencers whom you need to listen to. They're the ones who told us to reduce the weight of our filter. So, whether you're talking to someone in a store or online, the idea is the same. You must listen to what your consumers are saying. Having the product people actually want and need is key to success, but you won't know that if you aren't really listening. Today, all of our sales and marketing staff visit stores.

Then we priced to where we wanted to be. We knew the Sawyer Mini had the potential to disrupt the market. Keeping the price under twenty dollars. was essential to that disruption.

Aftershock: How Disruptors Listen

John Smith visited Haiti a few months after the 2010 earthquake. He traveled to a conference put on by the United Nations in the country's capital city, Port-au-Prince. The pressing need for clean water was a major topic of discussion. A number of other vendors and manufacturers were there besides Sawyer. Some had their own filters while others had chlorine tablets or similar treatments. Everyone was set up in a big circle inside a large ballroom. A wide variety of water cleaning and water filtering options were on display.

At this time in Sawyer's history, we were relatively unknown outside of the outdoor retail products market when it came to clean water. This earthquake was the first time our water filters received true international exposure. We were hearing that relief workers and NGOs were blown away by the simplicity and effectiveness of the Sawyer Squeeze. People were discovering that it is so much more than just a filter for hikers and campers out on the trail; it was a life-saving device.

While vendors were invited to attend the conference, John and the others were not invited to attend every meeting. One day, René Préval, then president of Haiti, was in a room nearby. After one of his meetings, the president and his entourage came into the ballroom to meet each vendor and take a few minutes to discuss their water treatment goods. He asked every vendor, "You are in Haiti. What water treatment system are you personally using?" John was told that each vendor got that deer-in-the-headlights look. Everyone, to a person, said, "Sawyer."

It was shocking. Even the guys with the chlorine tablets admitted to using Sawyer water filters. Nobody trusted the water, and so they were all drinking through Sawyer's portable water filters. John and I have long seen eye-to-eye on the importance of creating the best possible product. "'Good enough' is not good enough" is something we have said to each other for years and still say to this day. It's a way of continuing to push each other, and the whole Sawyer team, to create the very best products on the market. These incredible admissions were the results of our team's hard work. When people are in crisis, they will not settle for anything less than the best. So, why settle for manufacturing anything other than the best?

I don't share this story to be braggadocios. I'm obviously incredibly proud of Sawyer water filters, but pride isn't the point of this story. The 2010 earthquake in Haiti was at first only a natural disaster that we could respond to. But the response to the Sawyer Squeeze was like an aftershock that shifted our company's foundation. We were once primarily known as a manufacturer of insect repellents, sunscreens, and first aid kits. Then suddenly we were receiving international attention because we could provide an easy-to-use, easy-to-distribute, high-performance solution during a water crisis.

In this chapter, we've discussed the complexities of determining the cost of making one more widget. We've also been reminded that none of Sawyer's success would have come about if we had not first listened to the needs of our consumers and then invested in technology to meet those needs. John listened to our consumers' responses in real-time (in this case, competing vendors and manufacturers, leaders of NGOs, and Haitian officials), and we responded with the best that our technology could bring. From that point on, we factored in disaster relief efforts and the overall global water crisis into our manufacturing decisions about every Sawyer water filter. And we've used Incremental Variable Cost analysis all along the way to help us disrupt the water filter market.

Chapter Twelve
Think Big

When we moved Sawyer (then called Saffeta) from Illinois to Florida in May 1988, we were *small*. I was the only employee at the time. I did everything from assembling the product to shipping to answering the phone. We had inventory boxes all over the house. My older kids built forts out of them in the living room. We even stacked them up and threw their mattresses on top to be used as makeshift beds until we could buy bedframes. We moved to Florida to connect with Starmark, a company that made insect repellents and sunblock and who would private label them for us. We were basically starting over.

The Gulf War broke out in August 1990. Shortly after, a friend of mine at the military-related outdoors company, Brigade Quartermaster (known as BrigradeQM), told me about an opportunity to bid on manufacturing sunblock to be used by military personnel during Operation Desert Shield. The quantities were massive, something like 230,000 bottles per week. At the time, our manufacturing partner was only hand-filling up to two thousand bottles per day.

So, of course, I bid on it. We may have been a small operation, but we were thinking *big*. I remember going home for lunch and telling Barbara that we were going after the contract. She looked astonished, but she supported me.

We bid $0.69 per bottle while the next lowest bid was $1.99 per bottle. We kept asking ourselves what was missing (by this time, Starmark had hired all necessary employees), but our numbers didn't lie: we could do it for just $0.69. Naturally, we won the bid. But how were we actually going to fulfill these orders? Fortunately Ned Lyke, my financial investor and close friend, invested $800,000 in about fifteen minutes to secure all the components and equipment we needed. At the same time, we worked out a subcontracting arrangement with another manufacturer, Creative Cosmetics, Inc. (CCI), who would help us fulfill orders. The sunblock formula CCI used was spectacular, and, as I would learn later, it benefitted Sawyer for years to come.

It was amazing. Not only had we just secured a contract that dwarfed every other sale in our company's short history, but my investor had so much trust in me that he completely outfitted us in hardly any time at all! Saffeta (Sawyer) was about to have its best year ever!

Then the other shoe dropped.

We learned that to qualify for the bid we had to be a commercially sold brand. We had only gotten into the sunblock business *that month*. Up to that point, we had only shipped *two cases* of sunblock—just two! We were doomed to lose the contract, and I'd have to repay my friend Ned.

As God would have it, one of our two cases went to a small store in McAllen, Texas, called Broadway Hardware. This store was just one mile from the inspector's location. He took a short drive to the store, saw our sunblock sitting on the shelf, and called his superior to confirm that we qualified for the bid!

Orders began coming in and we went to work. We eventually manufactured 3.2 million bottles of sunblock and hit our cost estimates.

I believed in a big God before any of this happened. I knew God could do things like this. But rarely had I seen such an obvious display of his care in the details of our work. We had no idea who this inspector was or where he was located during this process. The fact that he was just down the road from one of only two stores *in the nation* that stocked our new sunblock was more than a coincidence. I could only assume that this was preordained by God. This instance, and many others, have taught me over and over again that if you have a big God, you can do big things. He will use you.

CCI became our sunblock supplier for many years after this contract ended. When their owner, Bill Shields, decided to sell the company, he transferred all supplies and formulas to us. That original sunblock formula is what we still use today in our Bonding Base Sunscreen. It now has a loyal, almost cult-like following. Additionally, after Operation Desert Shield ended, we bought Starmark. When it was all said and done, we had won a major government contract, fulfilled it spectacularly, and ended up with an amazing sunscreen formula. I do not take credit for how everything turned out. I have a big God.

***

In this chapter, I want to talk about *big* things. I want to talk about thinking *big* and doing *big*. We've spent most of this book talking about how to make a profit. We began by covering the core ideas for starting a business, as well as the culture-changing concept of Creative Destruction. We've discussed financing your business, managing your business, and tools you can use to make good decisions quickly. We then focused on the importance of building relationships with your vendors, retailers, and the end consumer. Finally, we've discussed some concepts that are not discussed as much as they need to be—like Math Trap, GMROIs, and Incremental Variable Cost—which will ensure that your business continues to grow.

But what is all of this for? Why do we put so much time and energy into growing our business? Sure, it's nice to have a full bank account. A healthy savings brings a sense of security with it. It's wonderful to reward your employees well. And who doesn't like to take a vacation every once in a while? Or drive a nice truck? But isn't there anything more?

We're going to talk about giving and changing the world one life at a time. It is no small dream or task to change the world. However, you'll be surprised that your business can do astronomically greater things than you can imagine when you think big and when you have a big God.

Why Give?

There are no U-Hauls in heaven. It's as simple as that. You can't take it with you, though many cultures across history have believed otherwise. The pharaohs of ancient Egypt were buried in pyramids filled with treasures because their people believed it would give them a more luxurious and comfortable afterlife. The tomb of Tutankhamen is a prime example. It was filled with textiles, jewelry, pottery, food, and even extra chariots. But centuries later, archaeologists revealed that the pharaoh's treasures were still there—sorry, King Tut—broken and disintegrating due to centuries of weather and looting. Think of how those treasures might have been used to help those living in Egypt at that time. Instead, they were hidden away, literally buried in the desert.

I sincerely hope that your business will grow and your profits will increase by employing the principles you've learned in this book. I hope your accounts are full and that your business booms. But I sincerely hope that you do *not* bury your treasures in the desert, literally or metaphorically. When it's time for you to meet your creator, you won't be able to take your wealth with you. So why not use it now? Why not learn a lesson from King Tut and use the money to change the lives of the living? Entombing it in a bank account doesn't do anyone any good.

How to Give

Now that you're convinced you want to give more away, what's the best way to do so? How does it actually work? My best piece of advice is to use current tax laws to maximize your giving potential. One good way is to give away your goods or services if you can. Sawyer makes water filters, insect repellents, and sunscreens. People need these items. So, we can donate them at a loss and not have to pay the taxes we would've incurred had we sold them. This magnifies your gift-giving by the level of your incremental tax bracket. Restaurants have food they can give away before taxes. Plumbers can do free plumbing services for needy people, etc.

Additionally, a legitimate expense we focus on R & D. Because we're publishing the data from our research, the cost of R & D is a legitimate expense. We work with the various schools I mentioned earlier, like Hope College, where we're funding a Global Health Initiative. We collect data that we publish in medical journals to verify our filters' worthiness.

Both Hope College and Messiah University send student athletes to teach sports to impoverished kids and install Sawyer water filters in their homes. Our contribution, both financially and with product, is tax deductible as a promotional expense as it stimulates a need that NGOs can address. Sometimes they even overlap with what our NGOs are doing. Those things are tax-deductible expenses.

It goes without saying that *you must not cheat on your taxes*. Here I'll turn again to the words of Jesus. He lived during a time when Rome occupied Israel. Jews were heavily taxed and oppressed, and they longed to be free of Roman rule. When Jesus was asked if it was necessary to pay taxes, he famously said, "Give back to Caesar what is Caesar's" (Matthew 22:21). In other words, yes, you have to pay your taxes. However, you can use all the legal deductions to only pay as much as you have to.

I'd rather be in charge of distributing our wealth than letting the government do it. Wouldn't you? By using tax laws to our advantage, we get to determine how more of our profits are

> **I'd rather be in charge of distributing our wealth than letting the government do it.**

donated and who ends up benefitting from them rather than paying most of it in taxes to the government, who may or may not use them for the world-changing programs we care about. (Probably not!)

The Process for Giving

Over the years, people have asked questions like, "Why does Sawyer do work around the world? Why not do more philanthropic work in the US? What makes you go to these far, unreached places?"

Sawyer does help in relief and philanthropic work in the US, though you may not be aware of it. We have tried to follow a biblical model for making an impact which is known as the Four Layer Ministry and Donations/Investments model. The idea is to begin locally and move outward until you've reached the whole world in a way that mirrors the spread of the gospel. The Christian church began in Jerusalem (what was "local" to Jesus and his first followers), then moved to the surrounding countryside of Judea, then to the neighboring foreign region of Samaria, and finally "to the ends of the earth" (Acts 1:8). Similarly, we do projects in our local county. Then we move to areas within the US and the surrounding regions, doing some of our best work in Canada and Mexico. And, of course, the projects you've read about throughout this book are overseas and in some of the most remote places in the world.

In the US, we have been a part of the relief effort for every hurricane since 2010. During natural disasters, we either donate or sell filters at an extreme discount to various NGOs to ensure that people have clean water. We also donate sunscreen and insect repellents. As we've said, there is no sense in trying to make maximum profit on every filter sold to every NGO, especially during a crisis. Not only would we sell fewer filters and thus prevent people from having access to clean water, but Sawyer benefits by having a higher volume of filters to produce. Remember the principle from the last chapter: every time you double your production, you reduce your cost by 20 percent. Sawyer has also supported relief efforts due to flooding in eastern Kentucky, as well as boil alerts in Jackson, Mississippi.

One of our staff members is a longtime friend of the award-winning guitarist and music producer Stevie Salas. Stevie has worked with virtually everyone, from Rod Stewart to Justin Timberlake, and has been recorded on more than seventy different albums. Stevie is also a proud Apache. Through our partnership with him and an NGO called Healthy Six Nations, we have worked together to bring clean water to First Nations in Canada. Healthy Six Nations purchased ten thousand discounted Sawyer Tap water filters to serve the Ontario First Nations Reservations.[47] Sawyer continues to play a big part in bringing clean water to First Nations in Canada. We also do similar work on several reservations in the US.

At the same time, we work on numerous projects in Mexico, including one with The Bucket Ministry focused on Ciudad Victoria (Victory City). TBM will distribute and conduct a study of three of our filter systems in this region: the Tap Filter, the Bucket System, and a filter on a soda bottle. The objec-

---

47 Health Nations has also released a documentary called *Boil Alert*. You can find it online if you want to learn more about the clean water crisis for First Nations tribes in Canada and elsewhere.

tive of this study is to show that all three systems yield similar health and economic improvements. All current published data revolves around the International Bucket System. However, the tap filter is a better solution in urban settings. This study will demonstrate its effectiveness and open doors for more strategic work in other urban settings like Ciudad Victoria. The filter on a bottle is by far the lowest cost and most economical system for disasters or small budgets. This study will also demonstrate how effective this simple, inexpensive solution can be for clean water problems.

With this data, we hope more governments will get involved with us. Preliminarily, we expect to show up to a 30 percent savings in the annual income of each family using a Sawyer water filter because they no longer need to purchase bottled water or use energy (which has a cost) to boil water. We expect this data to reveal that family members are taking fewer sick days from work and school too. We are forming a joint task force with leaders from the Organization of American States (OAS)[48] to integrate Sawyer water filters with some of their projects. We are funding a pilot project through one of our NGOs so OAS will have its own "proof of concept" data.

You have already read about how we have partnered with others to provide access to clean water in places like Liberia and Kenya. We started locally and moved globally, from our "Jeru-

---

[48] OAS is a union of pan-America first established in 1890. Its purpose is "to strengthen peace and security in the hemisphere; promote representative democracy; ensure the peaceful settlement of disputes among members; provide for common action in the event of aggression; and promote economic, social, and cultural development." "About the OAS," accessed February May 29, 2024, https://usoas.usmission.gov/our-relationship/about-oas/.

salem," to Honduras, to Haiti, to the Marshall Islands, and to wherever access to clean water is needed. The question to ask yourself is: *What needs could my business meet if we started locally and then moved globally?* Think *big*. How many lives could your company potentially change? Sometimes you only have to create a model or an example to inspire other businesses to join you.

More Than an Outdoor Company

The more you give, the more opportunities you'll find to give. Some will be bad. An NGO or nonprofit may not have their act together, or the ROI on your gift may not be optimal. But some opportunities aren't bad; they just don't make sense for your company to participate in. It has made perfect sense for Sawyer to become actively involved with NGOs fighting the global water crisis. They were already using our water filters because of their effectiveness. Many of these NGOs have moved through The Circle of Customers from fringe to loyal. In fact, we no longer think of them as customers, but as partners.

But there are a lot of other needs in the world aside from clean water. It doesn't always make intuitive or strategic sense for Sawyer to take an active role, even when the needs are great. The more we gave to clean water efforts, the more we wanted to start a foundation. In 2021, after years of discussion and thought, the Sawyer Foundation officially became a 501(c)(3) nonprofit. The Sawyer Foundation is built on three pillars: university-level global health and education and research, transformational community development, and providing relief in disaster situations. Importantly, the foundation also allows us to participate in projects that are worthy of our investment and energy but may not be directly involved with water.

For example, in April 2021, we began partnering with a non-profit organization called Man Up and Go, which focuses on helping fatherless kids break out of various destructive cycles that often lead to addiction, imprisonment, or worse. Through the foundation, Sawyer donated to an initiative that helps foster kids who have aged out of the foster care system increase their digital proficiency skills, which in turn helps them build their résumés and find better employment.

It's important to note here that providing these kids with a chance for digital proficiency is not tax deductible for Sawyer. It isn't part of our R & D efforts or in any other way something we could claim on our taxes as a deduction. So, we take the money and instead give it to the foundation (where we get the tax savings) and then the foundation can donate it to Man Up and Go or whatever organization we're working with.

So, the Sawyer Foundation is doubly important. It gives us an avenue for donating to life-changing causes that have nothing to do with clean water. It also allows us to save on our taxes so we can continue giving more away. (This is another example of being in charge of how your wealth is given away rather than the government.)

The foundation also allows outside donors to know that 100 percent of their donation goes to clean water projects and not overhead expenses. All overhead expenses, which are quite minimal, are paid for by Sawyer.

While the foundation began in 2021, we didn't start actively taking donations from outside donors until 2023. For the first two years, Sawyer Products was the only donor to The Sawyer

Foundation. In 2023, some of our social media partners started to raise awareness about the clean water efforts in places like Kibera through their influential videos. These partners (gifted storytellers like Dan Becker and others) naturally wanted to give back. They challenged their audiences to donate too—and the audience showed up! Enter the foundation. The foundation receives these donations—which, as of this writing, are almost always designated for clean water efforts—and tracks *exactly* how the money is spent. This allows us to guarantee every donor that 100 percent of their money is going to the effort they are giving to.

In its short history, most of the Sawyer Foundation's donations have gone to clean water efforts. Less than 10 percent of the foundation's internal donations (i.e., donations from Sawyer Products to the Sawyer Foundation) go to strategic initiatives other than clean water, while 100 percent of all external donations go to clean water efforts (which, at the time of this writing, are the only efforts we have received external money for). These things may change in future years as the Sawyer Foundation grows. We may find other strategic efforts to donate more time and money toward. (For example, beginning in 2024, the Sawyer Foundation will donate to veteran groups that take wounded veterans on outdoor trips.) Regardless of the cause, we could not be as effective in our giving without the Sawyer Foundation. It provides levels of both flexibility and accountability that Sawyer Products could not provide on its own.

Investing in Future Generations

"There's this moment when the crowd starts to rise to their feet. It's natural and it's so cool to be a part of."

These are the words of Aaron Faro, Associate Head Coach and Athletics Recruitment Coordinator at Messiah University. Aaron is a gifted athlete who has played in and coached countless games that caused fans to rise to their feet. But this story is not about a sporting event.

"We do our filter demonstrations with very basic, clear buckets," Aaron continued. "We pull the water directly from their water source. We will sometimes even add dirt to it so they can see how dirty the water is. The buckets look like a mud puddle. Then we filter this same water into a clear bottle. The bottle is often down low and the people are usually sitting. As the bottle starts to fill, people stand up so they can see better. But then the ones behind them can't see so they stand up and pretty soon the whole group is crowded around the filter.

"They're so honed in on it! They're even startled as they see clean, clear water from their own water source for the first time. It's a powerful experience."

Since 2011, Sawyer has been working with Aaron and Messiah University to send student athletes on sports-based ministry trips through a program called AROMA. Aaron is the director. He has traveled to numerous foreign countries that lack the resources of the Western world, teaching various sports and training people who live with dirty water how to use Sawyer water filters.

Aaron recalled that "one of the most memorable trips was when our wrestling coach traveled with us to a small community outside Santo Domingo, Dominican Republic." This village had a pigpen right near the location where Aaron's team would do the water filter training. The pen, as you can imagine, was a mess of mud, food scraps, and animal waste.

"One of our students asked a local community leader what would happen if they drank the water from the pig pen. The community leader responded, 'You will die.' So, our coach just marched over and dug water right out of the muddy puddles the pigs were standing in. Then he proceeded to filter it and took a big gulp in front of everyone! It was one of the more shocking demonstrations I remember. Even some of our students [who were trained in the effectiveness of the filters] had to check themselves. Like, do we *really* believe it's going to be alright?"

The AROMA program has so far sent students on more than seventy-five trips to over twenty different countries. More than 1,500 students, coaches, and alumni have participated in these life-changing trips, and there is no sign of stopping. Aaron's vision has always been to get Messiah's athletes out into their local communities and on international trips, where they can use sports to build relationships and share their faith. He believes in the value of cross-cultural work to expand a student's worldview.

But international trips are obviously expensive. Aaron started AROMA in 2009 but could only equip students to participate in local sports ministry programs. Without knowing Aaron, I began speaking with the Director of Development at Messiah University in early 2011 about ways to expose students to the needs of the world. My daughters had graduated from Messiah, and I wanted to do more for the next generation with the resources I had. (Remember, you can't take it with you.) At that time, Aaron was actively praying for the opportunity to take students on international trips.

"I almost dropped the phone when my boss called me," Aaron said. "He starts telling me about someone who wants to develop a program that will give all of our athletes the opportunity to go on international sports ministry trips and asks, 'Do I think we could do that?'"

Aaron thinks big and puts his faith in a big God. To suddenly receive the donations he'd been praying for "felt very out of the blue in some ways . . . and yet, I've been following God for a long time and so I'm also not shocked at anything that he does." We began to work with Aaron that spring, and by the summer of 2011, he had organized two trips overseas with students who would teach sports, share their faith, and teach people how to use our water filters. The AROMA program has flourished in the intervening years, leading many students to pursue careers in various fields of cross-cultural relief work.

I do not take credit for the good things that have come out of the AROMA program. No one at Sawyer does, and even Aaron does not take the credit. But together, Sawyer and Messiah University have been able to change the lives of countless people—the student athletes, the coaches, and all of those who now have access to clean water. Why? Because we think *big* and we believe in a *big* God.

We now have a similar program at Hope College called SEED. Like the AROMA program, we are excited to see students' lives change as they encounter the needs of the world.

Thinking big can turn pig slop into drinking water. It can create moments like the one Aaron described when a crowd breathlessly rises to its feet with the realization that they can have clean water! What kind of moments can you create by thinking big?

> **What kind of moments can you create by thinking big?**

The Little Boy with the Lunch

My wife, Barbara, was once asked to describe Sawyer. She said, "I feel like we're the little boy with a lunch. You come to the Lord with a little bit and he's able to use it in such bigger and grander ways than you ever could have imagined."

I love that description. Barbara is referring to the famous story of Jesus feeding five thousand people. It's a story about how God miraculously provided for people in need. Jesus started with limited physical resources—a small lunch of two fish and five loaves of bread—that were given to him in faith by a small boy. By the power of God, Jesus took this meager amount of food and fed five thousand people. The people were so well fed that twelve baskets of extra food were left over.[49]

I see my work at Sawyer, and your work at your business, as an opportunity to be like the boy in this story. The Bible doesn't record much information about him. He's not the main character in the story; Jesus is. But the boy was a good steward with what he had. He had a small amount of food in a vast crowd of hungry people. So, he trusted Jesus to take these resources and do something big. And Jesus did.

I want to be a good steward of what I have—what a whole team of incredible people have helped build—at Sawyer. And then I want to trust that God will do something big and miraculous with it.

In this book, I've tried to share the best of what I know about growing a business. This "Sawyer Think" is how I have tried to be a good steward over Sawyer. Practicing future thinking, focus-

---

49 Read the full story in the Bible in John 6:1–15.

ing on Creative Destruction, listening to our customers, turning our customers into partners, and considering the whole picture of every decision—each of these is an act of stewardship. The stories I've shared in each chapter are evidence that God is using what resources we have to change people's lives. After forty years at Sawyer, it is still hard to believe all that has happened.

I am far from being a perfect person, but I have faith in a big God—the kind of God who miraculously changes lives and will do so on a scale we can't even imagine when we act in faith, like the little boy with the lunch. Though I always practice future thinking (and I encourage you to do the same), there are aspects to the future that are way beyond my comprehension. But we will go full throttle to wherever God takes Sawyer.

As I write this book, our team has been focused on new opportunities with the tap filter. It promises to be our most important product yet. Our International Bucket System usually filters twenty to forty gallons of water a day to meet a family or a group of families' needs. For even less money, the tap filter can filter up to *five hundred* gallons of water per day. Both can last for ten or more years. So, for as little as ten cents, we can give a person ten years of safe water. *Any* tap in the world can be made safe instantly. Therefore, we believe that God has even bigger plans for us ahead.

What does the future look like for your organization? Could God somehow "feed the five thousand" with your business? Can you take all that you've learned in this book and use it to manage your company more wisely? As you do so, can you offer your resources to God—your two fish and five loaves—so he can help a crowd of needy people?

As an entrepreneur, business owner, or business leader, you have an opportunity. What will you do with it? Have a big God and you can do big things. He will use you.

How big is your God?

Acknowledgments

Anybody who knows me knows that I do not have a command of the art of writing. I live in the math world, so we must acknowledge the ghostwriter Andy Rogers and my agent Tom Dean for converting my ideas into communicative English.

As you know, it takes many people and key events to come together to make a person's life what it is. Some of the pivotal points in my life were getting a George F. Baker scholarship to attend Northwestern Graduate School of Management (now called Kellogg) and, from there, getting a job in the General Electric Strategy Planning unit. This program was put together by Jack Welch in order to bring in MBA grads to shake up "GE think." That we did, or at least we tried.

From there, I gained some valuable marketing experiences with the consumer product companies of Weed Eater, Poulan chainsaws, and SKIL Power Tools. These experiences gave me the incentive to start Sawyer.

Needless to say, Sawyer has been quite the ride. Without the support of my wife, Barbara, I am afraid Sawyer would not have happened. How many men get to come home and say they are going to quit a promising corporate career to start a company selling snake bite kits and the wife with three kids and a fourth on the way says, "OK"? Barbara is a treasure, and I am blessed to share this life with her. And the four kids have been fun too.

It goes without saying that God has had his hand on me my whole life and certainly has had his hand on Sawyer. As you read in the book, God engineered big events at Sawyer more than once.

During the course of running Sawyer through both tough and blessed times, I developed my own internal training program called Grasshopper U (as in, "You have much to learn, Grasshopper," from *Kung Fu*). These lessons were developed for our workers, summer interns, and select associates.

People have been on my case for years to get these lessons in book form so, despite my years of resistance, I acquiesced. The last bit of encouragement came from Dr. Esther Choy at the Northwestern Kellogg School of Management. Having met her at one of my reunions, she taught us her IRS system of communicating: intriguing beginning, riveting middle, and a satisfying ending. Hopefully, we captured some of those principles in this book. We'll see how she grades us.

Obviously, many people went unmentioned but not forgotten. We hope you, the reader, will find some helpful pieces and business tidbits, as well as encouragement to make the world a better place than when you found it.

About the Authors

Kurt Avery is the founder of Sawyer Products and currently serves as president and owner. Founded in 1984, Sawyer has been at the forefront of innovation in water filtration, insect repellent, sunscreen, and first aid. He is passionate about and committed to creating disease-free water for life in communities throughout the world. Kurt is a graduate of Hope College and Northwestern Kellogg School of Management. He and his wife, Barbara, are parents of four and grandparents of five. They reside in Florida.

A. L. Rogers is a ghostwriter, editor, author, and writing coach. Andy joined the book industry in 2007 and published his first book in 2017. He has worked on hundreds of successful book projects in a variety of roles for major publishing houses, independent publishers, and nonprofit organizations. Andy and his family live in Grand Rapids, Michigan.

Glossary

brand equity – The commercial value of your brand based on the consumer's perception of your brand name

causal effects – The relationship between variables, specifically, asking *how much of* B will change A

Circle of Customers – A diagram for understanding the core marketing principle of building your business by selling more things to the same people (See Appendix C)

Creative Destruction – An idea popularized by Joseph Schumpeter: Industries destroy and recreate themselves from within through innovative developments, often achieved by entrepreneurs who introduce something revolutionary, or due to changes in laws, technology, or social norms.

Decision Matrix – A decision-making tool that helps you address every variable in a given decision. It helps you avoid making decisions based on variables you may be overly or emotionally focused on. It also helps you make good decisions more quickly. (See Appendix A)

Economies of Scale – Proportionate savings in your cost based on increased production. Summed up by this core economic idea: each time you double your production, you reduce your cost by 20 percent.

full line – A retail strategy that involves purchasing related but less profitable items to create the perception of a complete department to increase sales of the most profitable items

good, better, best – A strategy used in both pricing and sales that involves creating three tiers of products or prices and using products one and three to sell product two

GMROI – (/G/IM-roy) Gross Margin Return on Investment. A formula for approaching sales that maximizes your retailer's profit. A = Retail price. B = The retailer's landed cost. C = The number of units sold that year on that peg. D = The number of units in the pipeline, which represents the retailer's total investment. E = The footprint of your product in the retail store. For a simple analysis, use 1.

$$\frac{(A-B) \times C}{B \times D \times E}$$

hockey stick – A forecast that predicts reversing declines into continued growth. It looks like a hockey stick.

Incremental Variable Cost – Your cost for making one more unit based on a number of variables, including raw materials, direct labor, indirect costs, and Fully Absorbed Costs. (See Appendix E)

Math Trap – A fundamental concept for strategic thinking based on understanding the relationship between numerators and denominators

open-to-buy – An inventory management strategy retailers use to calculate how many products they can purchase for a specific period; an investment management tool

present value – The value of goods or services in today's dollars in contrast to a future value which could be affected by a number of variables, including inflation and profit goals

purchase order (PO) – A commitment by a buyer to purchase a good or service from a supplier

shiny object – A design element—a band of distinct color, a sunburst, etc.—that steals the consumer's attention from other products

trade equity – Your relational "stock" with your trade partners; the value of your relationship with them based on your shared history

violator – A word or a point of emphasis placed at a slight diagonal on product packaging

Appendices

Appendix A: Decision Matrix

Appendix B: Life Cycle Curves

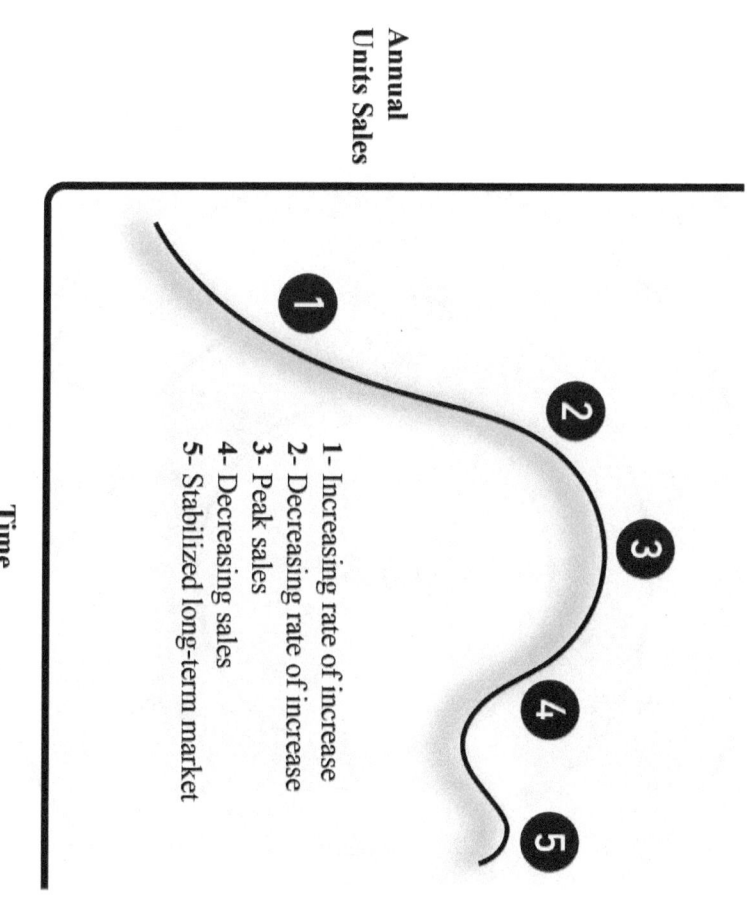

1- Increasing rate of increase
2- Decreasing rate of increase
3- Peak sales
4- Decreasing sales
5- Stabilized long-term market

Appendix C: The Circle of Customers

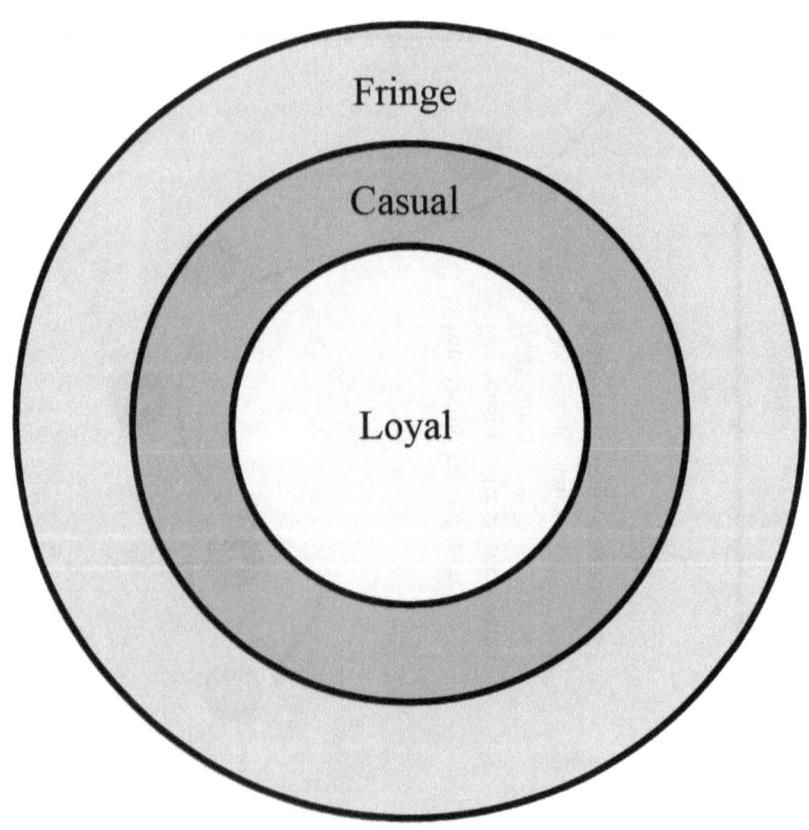

Appendix D: Direct Cost Curve

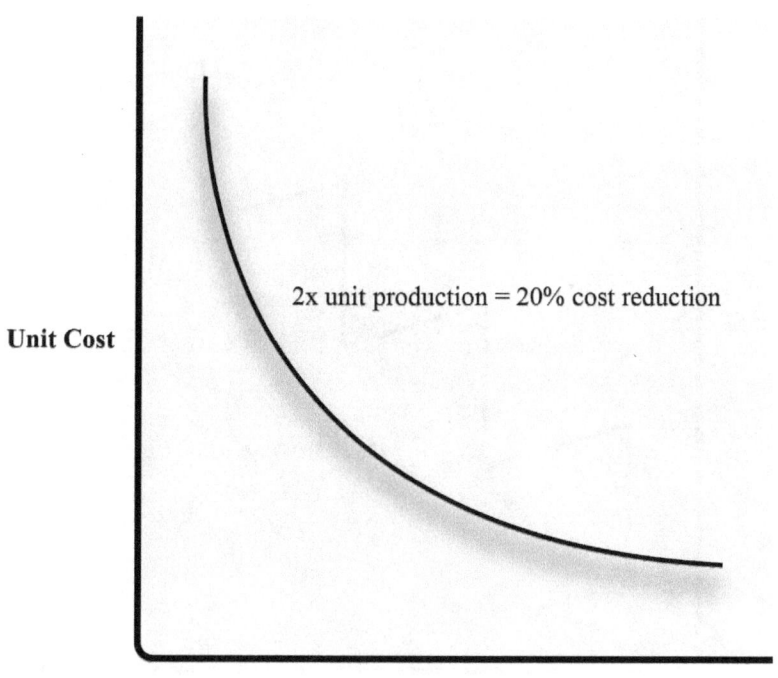

Appendix E: Incremental Variable Cost

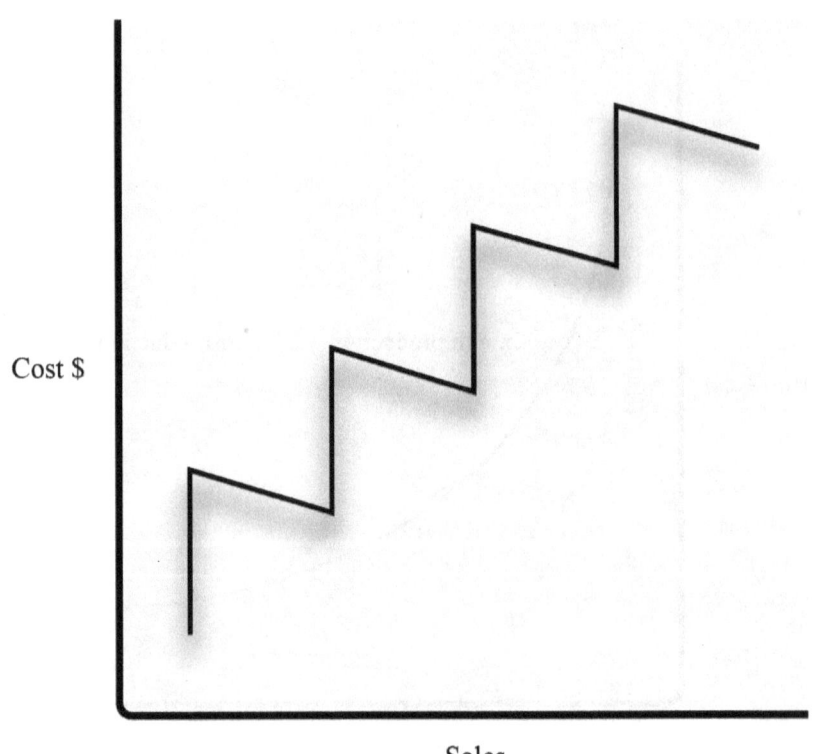

A free ebook edition is available with the purchase of this book.

To claim your free ebook edition:

1. Visit MorganJamesBOGO.com
2. Sign your name CLEARLY in the space
3. Complete the form and submit a photo of the entire copyright page
4. You or your friend can download the ebook to your preferred device

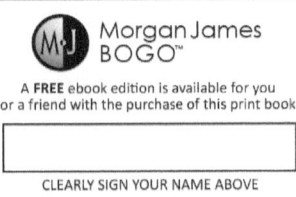

Print & Digital Together Forever.

Snap a photo   Free ebook   Read anywhere

www.ingramcontent.com/pod-product-compliance
Lightning Source LLC
Chambersburg PA
CBHW020858180526
45163CB00007B/2555